The

RESULTS!

FORMULA

Why Goals
Don't Work
and
Results Do!

JEAN OURSLER

Interior Book Design and Illustrations: D2 Studios Inc.

Printed in the United States of America.

FIRST EDITION

978-1-945853-11-1

Marriah
Publishing

DEDICATION

To Janice Oursler who instilled in me from a very young age the importance of always knowing the results you want on a one-year, five-year and ten-year basis so you can achieve them.

Thanks Mom for being the wind beneath my wings!

TABLE OF CONTENTS

INTRODUCTION vii

CHAPTER 1 GOODBYE GOALS 1

CHAPTER 2 HELLO RESULTS................................. 21

CHAPTER 3 CAVEMAN BRAIN™ 33

CHAPTER 4 GET COMFORTABLE BEING UNCOMFORTABLE.... 57

CHAPTER 5 OTHER PEOPLE'S BAGGAGE 75

CHAPTER 6 RESULTS MINDSET................................ 87

CHAPTER 7 Z TO A RESULTS THINKER...................... 99

CHAPTER 8 READY... 113

CHAPTER 9 END.. 127

CHAPTER 10 STEPS.. 141

CHAPTER 11 YOU 153

CHAPTER 12 LEVELS OF LEARNING 167

CHAPTER 13 TRANSFORMATION........................... 177

CHAPTER 14 SUCCESS.. 187

CHAPTER 15 YOUR NEXT STEPS ON YOUR RESULTS JOURNEY 199

THE LAST WORDS FROM JEAN, THE RESULTS QUEEN®............ 205

ACKNOWLEDGEMENTS....................................... 207

JEAN'S BIO AND CONTACT INFORMATION........................ 209

INTRODUCTION

Having goals has been hammered into all of us as THE thing that makes us successful. However, what I have seen from working with my clients is goals do not make them successful. What make them successful are RESULTS.

If you have heard me speak, watched my TV show, Get More Results, sat through one of my workshops or been a client, you have heard my mantra, "Give up goals to get results!" If this `concept is new to you, this book highlights why I firmly believe RESULTS win over GOALS every time. I'm sure you are saying, "Wait, aren't they the same thing?" I don't think they are and that is why I wrote this book.

Here's what I found out about the goal process in working with my clients, everyone believes they should have them, yet there are many people who never set goals, and for those that do, few get accomplished. I think it is time for more of us to achieve what we want to achieve. I think it is time to get results by giving up goals. The reason? I think goals only work for a few of us. I know results can work for all of us!

Think about it. Do you talk about goals? Do you talk about results? Do you talk about both or do you talk about neither? How many of us talk about results? How does talking about goals make us more successful? I don't think it does. I think talking about and working toward RESULTS make us more successful. I am on a mission to get everyone to give up goals because I believe setting goals just doesn't work. I encourage every person I come in contact with who is serious about living a successful life to focus on what does work. Focus on results.

I am sure you are wondering how changing one little word could make you more successful because there are many examples of people who have set goals and achieved them. How does changing the word goal to the word results really make a difference? For many of us it does, and in this book, I will explain how it makes a difference.

Results have been my number one priority since I started my company. For me it began as a theory, but soon I saw concrete evidence as I coached my clients through the Results Formula. They became more successful when they set results, visualized the results and implemented the formula. This was true for those who did not write down goals. It was absolutely true for those who had written down their goals but couldn't achieve them.

Why do you think I am called The Results Queen®? Actually, my clients crowned me The Results Queen; they said they had accomplished more working with me than working by themselves or with others. They were amazed by the results they achieved, and that got me thinking. What was I doing or saying that made such a difference? I wondered if it had anything to do with my "bottom line" focus. Was that the key? Was this "bottom line" focus what caused my clients to turn a corner and the reason for both my success and theirs? I concluded it was and it still is.

When I work with a client, the first question I ask is, "what results do you want to achieve?" Not, "what are your goals?" In fact, I have never asked my clients about their goals because I know goals don't work.

I realize this may be a radical departure from what you have been told. I think it is those disruptive, radical departures that make us more successful. If you want to be more successful and are tired of getting the same old same old, then I invite you to turn the page and start focusing on getting results by giving up your goals.

To Your RESULTS!

Jean

The Results Queen®

CHAPTER 1

GOODBYE GOALS

*"When you think and focus on results, then
you will get the results you think and focus on."*

Jean, The Results Queen®

Depending on what research you read, there are numerous articles that state something like five percent of people create goals and only two percent actually write their goals down. Those are pretty low numbers. I guess the theory is when you create goals and write them down you are more likely to achieve them.

How many goals have you achieved? Are you part of the five percent? Are you part of the two percent? Are you in the 95 percent group who don't set goals? I want you to understand being a part of the 95 percent is not a bad thing. Just like those in the five percent group who do have goals is a good thing. For me, there isn't any good or bad; there is just what works for you. If goal setting and goal achieving are working for you, stop reading and move on. If that system isn't working for you, then read on.

If goals really worked, wouldn't more of us participate in setting and achieving them? With numbers like five percent (or in some cases two percent), you have to wonder if this goal-setting/achieving process is a hidden secret to success many of us are just ignoring. If goals are that important to success, then what is preventing the rest of us from actually setting and achieving them?

I believe there are a host of explanations as to why more of us are not participating in the goal process. See if any of these resonates with you.

- We try to set goals, and we get distracted and never get back to them.
- We try to set goals, and then we give up.
- It's too much work to set goals, so why even try?
- What happens when we don't achieve those goals?
- Won't we be a failure if we don't achieve our goals?
- Most of us don't want to be a failure, right, so why even start?
- Why try if I am just going to fail?

And the list goes on.

For many of us, we just don't see the value in the goal process. Why? I believe it is due to the experiences we have had in the past. These experiences often happen because the process is negative and fraught with pitfalls. Based on these previous experiences, we think, if there is nothing positive about the goal process experience, why would I want to participate in it again?

Even worst, imagine if we have been forced to participate in the goal process and it wasn't a great experience. If you are forced to participate in the goal process, for most of us, that just makes us want to participate in the process even less. Think about it, who wants to be forced to participate in anything, and if you are forced, how well do you do the activity? Of course, if there is an incentive we believe is important, we may choose to participate.

Here is one last exercise that points out just how negative the goal process can be for many of us. Say the word "goal" out loud. How do you feel when you say that word?

Now say the word "result" out loud. How do you feel when you said that word?

Let's try it one more time. Say the word "goal" again out loud. Now say the word "result." Can you hear the difference? Can you feel the difference? When my clients do this exercise, most of them feel more positive about the word "result" than the word "goal."

Why? When you say the word "goal," normally your voice goes down. When you say the word "result," normally your voice goes up. Our brains perceive a word that goes up as more positive. Our brains perceive a word that goes down as more negative. What do you think you respond better to – negative or positive? Most of us like the positive and will avoid the negative.

As long as we perceive goals are negative, we are going to continue to ensure we don't set goals or use goals unless we do something to make goals more positive. Most of us aren't even going down that path to make goals more positive, and even if we wanted to, most of us wouldn't know how.

I can hear you say, "Wait a minute, Jean. I never said goals were negative." Of course, you didn't. That is because you are saying it on a subconscious level. Before I confuse you, let me explain.

There is the conscious level and the subconscious level. Most of us think we operate on a conscious level. The opposite is true. Most of our thoughts and behaviors happen at a subconscious level and then move to a conscious level. There are lots of times we do things and don't understand why we did them. When that happens, you are operating on a subconscious level.

Not setting goals is operating on a subconscious level. Writing goals is operating on a conscious level. If you are in the majority of those who do not write down goals, you now know why. Now you can understand those thoughts because you've moved those thoughts from the subconscious to the conscious.

Another reason I don't use the word "goal" is that in my opinion, it gives you too much wiggle room for not accomplishing them. It is too easy not to follow through. When I hear people say, "this is my goal," it sounds to me that if you didn't achieve it, then you would be ok with it. Think about it. How many times have you said, "this is my goal" and actually achieved your goal versus "this is my goal" and didn't achieve it?

I often find when I have my clients say, "this is the result I am going to get," they actually achieve the results. I find this statement much more powerful. The reason why I think it is a more powerful statement is that it requires a commitment of purpose.

I believe that when you are working toward a result, you can visualize it better. When you can see something, then you can achieve it. Visualization techniques are very important in achieving results. I will talk about these techniques later in the book.

Another thing about working toward a result is when you encounter obstacles, and you will, I think it is easier to get around them because you know what the result is. With a goal, I think maneuvering around these obstacles is a lot harder because there is often no visualization and therefore when you encounter an obstacle, you stop because you haven't thought through what it will take to eliminate these obstacles.

If you have conquered every goal you set out to achieve, then it is clear, the goal process is working for you. As I have said before, if it works for you, then keep doing it. However, if you don't even set goals, let alone achieve every goal you set, then how well is the goal process working for you? If it doesn't work for you, then let's find the thing that does work…RESULTS!

It is time to give up goals and get RESULTS! What do I mean by that? I think we can all agree the goal process isn't working for 95 percent of us. So, what will work? What will help us achieve greater success? The answer is RESULTS!

How does focusing on results make us more successful? For some reason, our brains find it easier to navigate toward a result. We know the action steps we need to take. When obstacles arise, we figure out how to get around them. If it is something we truly want, we don't give up on our result. We keep working toward it no matter how long it takes. I find my clients work harder to obtain a result than a goal. It is like they can see the end, so they keep pushing themselves to get there.

I believe we honed this behavior when we were kids. Think about it. How many times do you see a kid in the store working on their parent or grandparent to get what they want? That kid is relentless in their efforts. They beg. They promise. They whine. They cry. They even will escalate to a temper tantrum. The bottom line is that that kid doesn't give up!

Think about when you wanted to buy a new car or a house or an

Xbox? When you want a result, you are most likely unstoppable. Just like the kid in the store. When you have a goal, it seems more allusive, and you most likely get distracted and lose interest. That is why 95% of us don't ever achieve our goals.

How do I know this? It is based on my interactions with my clients. Many of my clients show up on my doorstep without any goals and feel guilty because they think they should have them. Other clients who show up with goals are frustrated because they can't achieve them. I have other clients who have never even set a goal and wonder why they aren't more successful.

The first step with my new clients is transitioning them from goal focus to results focus. I ask them to give up on goals and focus on the results they want to achieve. When I say that, there is a switch that goes on in their heads. They can't list the goals they want to achieve, but they can list the results they want to achieve. One of my clients told me this technique makes you switch from goal setting to results getting.

How does this switch make results getting more achievable? They find it easier to figure the action steps needed to get these results. If they hit an obstacle, they work themselves around it, over it or straight through it because they had had a ton of practice getting results before they ever got to my doorstep. What they needed is a way to reframe their goal thinking to results thinking so they can tap back into those results-getting abilities. Those abilities they honed as kids but seem to have forgotten as adults.

Remember my clients were all kids at one time. They were the ones working their parents at the toy store to get the thing they really wanted. They didn't sit home organizing their wish list into goals. Think about it. How many kids do you see setting goals?

When did you learn the goal-setting process? There may have been people in your lives that talked about goals. Things like going to college or winning a game or getting good grades, but when did you learn a goal setting process?

Goal setting often has a lot of negative consequences. I think this is due to the way Corporate America has "enforced" goal setting. How many of us have had a bad experience with the goal setting process at our jobs? Usually the answer is, a lot of us. I think that is why many of us don't set goals.

I also think that the goal setting process is just not inherent to our nature. As humans, I believe we are wired for results. I don't think we are wired for goal setting which is why it doesn't come as easy as results getting. Goals seem to be about talking. Results, for me, is about action.

The challenge many of my clients have is that if they give

something up, they think they are failures. So what do they do? They keep doing the same thing hoping for different results. That is the definition of insanity. I am going to say this over and over again.

Getting rid of something that doesn't work is not failing. It is opening up yourself to new opportunities. Once my clients give up on the whole goal-setting process, they are more open to embracing a new way, the results way.

Please say this out loud: "I am giving up goals, and I'm getting results." Say it one more time: "I am giving up goals and getting results." Doesn't that feel good? Listen to the words. Is your voice going up at the end? I bet it is. Because that is what my clients say. Remember when your voice goes up, you sound more positive and the more positive it is, the more likely you are to do it.

Now that you are about getting results, what's the process? How are you going to achieve your results? I am going to discuss The RESULTS Formula starting in the next chapter. That is the key to get the results you want. However, I know some of you would like some pre-work to help you. I am going to give you my five step pre-work process I walk my clients through. This pre-work will help you when you start implementing the RESULTS Formula.

Ok, I can hear some of you say, "Jean, I don't want to do any pre-work." For those of you who like pre-work, here it is. For those of you who don't like pre-work, then I am going to ask you if you really want to change. If you do, then embrace the pre-work. It will help you.

FIVE STEP PRE-WORK PROCESS

1. Define the result you want.

I ask my clients what do they want to achieve? The list can be one result or a hundred.

2. Get the result out of your head and on paper

I require that they write each result down. Getting it out of your head makes a big difference in achieving the result. Why? Keeping it in your head can prevent you from obtaining the result you want. I have a saying. When you put it down on paper, it makes it real. I always think it is important to get the information out of your head and down on paper. I am not sure why this works, but what I find is that putting it on paper makes it real. Once it is real, then you can start working on achieving it. Saying it out loud is the first step in this process. Writing down is the ultimate step.

3. **Define the action steps, and then write them down.**

    I ask my clients to think about the action steps it takes to achieve the result(s). Most of us never think about the specific steps to achieve the result we want. It is important to be able to visualize what those steps look like and see yourself doing them in order to achieve them. Once you visualize your action steps, then get them down on paper.

4. **List what obstacles could occur along the results path.**

    First, my clients figure out what obstacles could happen as they are on their RESULTS journey. Next, my clients define what it will take to get through these obstacles. Defining the obstacles will help you know them when you see them. Having a plan before these obstacles happen will help you get through them when they occur. There may be one big obstacle or hundreds of small obstacles. It doesn't matter. What matters is that you list them and figure out what you will do to get through them. Whatever the number, they are now defined, and there is a plan for working through them.

5. **Implementation**

    The hard work is done. You have everything on paper that can assist you in achieving the results you want. Now it is time to put the plan into place. You can use

The RESULTS Formula to help you achieve these results.

Using this process, I find my clients can finally visualize the results they want. They can see themselves achieving the results before they ever physically achieve them. In using this system, my clients are willing to work harder to overcome the obstacles that come along the way because they know what they are working toward…RESULTS!

I am sure you are asking yourself, "how can changing that one simple word from goals to results make such a difference in one's life?" I believe the word change does something in our brains. I believe we are hardwired to achieve results. Look at us from when we were kids. There is always something that is pushing us to get the thing we want. I am not sure if we are hardwired to achieve goals. I do know we are hardwired to get results.

My clients are amazed at how a simple act of giving up goals can open up a whole world of achieving results. That's why I believe we should give up goals. It is why I know you need to start working toward results… now!

If you choose to start this process (and I hope you will), I want you only to focus on no more than five results. Why? Research shows our brains can only focus on up to five things at once.

If you are not getting the results you want to achieve, my question to you is how many things are on your list? If it is more than five, you need to pare that list down. You can work on three to five things short term or three to five things long term. It doesn't matter. What matters is it is no more than five. That is it.

Can you focus on less that five? Of course! I actually follow the rule of three. For some reason, things always come up in threes for me. Start noticing how many things comes in a group of three. I don't why this happens, but I do know that 3 priorities seem to work for many of my clients. In any event, it is up to you as long as it is not more than five priorities at a time.

Here is another thing that I hope will help you. At the end of each chapter, is a place for you to stop and write down what you want to implement from the chapter you just read. I call this section "Get Results Now! Steps." Hey, I am The Results Queen. I am all about getting results, and I will take every opportunity to get you there. These "Get Results Now! Steps" will help you on the path to achieving more results.

👑 GET RESULTS NOW! STEPS

1. **Stop speaking about goals.**

    When you hear yourself say the word goal, stop yourself and repeat the sentence again, this time using the word result. No matter where you are or whom you are with, make sure to monitor the way you speak about results. I can bet you say "my goal is" or "I am working on this goal" a lot.

2. **Make a list of the three to five results you want to achieve, and set a time period of when you want to achieve them.**

    Some of you will choose to achieve your results in one day, while others will choose one week. Some of you will pick 30 or 60 days. Others may pick a year, three years or even five. The time period is up to you. For my clients, I ask them to work in 90 day time periods. I just find it is easier for them to visualize because it is not too far out and it is just enough time to get the activity completed. I also like it because it coincides with the four quarters of the year. It is your choice. I have given you space to write this information.

    (Use Next Page)

Result #1_____ Time Frame_____

Result #2_____ Time Frame_____

Result #3_____ Time Frame_____

Result #4_____ Time Frame_____

Result #5_____ Time Frame_____

3.   **For each result you have written, develop the action steps you need to achieve the result.**

Result #1 Action Steps

_____

_____

_____

Result #2 Action Steps

_____

_____

_____

Result #3 Action Steps

_____

_____

_____

Result #4 Action Steps

_____

_____

_____

Result #5 Action Steps

_____

_____

_____

4. **Write down the obstacles you know you will encounter for each result. This way when you do encounter them, and you know you will, you will already know how to overcome them.**

Result #1 Obstacles and How I Will Get Through Them

_____

_____

_____

Result #2 Obstacles and How I Will Get Through Them

_____

_____

_____

Result #3 Obstacles and How I Will Get Through Them

_____

_____

_____

Result #4 Obstacles and How I Will Get Through Them

_____

_____

_____

Result #5 Obstacles and How I Will Get Through Them

_____

_____

_____

5. **You now have a working plan to get results.**

   You are ready to start putting The RESULTS Formula into action! Turn the page so you can learn this formula to help you achieve the results you want now and always.

CHAPTER 2

HELLO RESULTS

"Do you work toward a result or do you just go?"

Jean, The Results Queen®

My passion in life is to help others be more successful tomorrow than they are today. That's why I have developed the RESULTS Formula. This formula is your master key to becoming more oriented to achieving results. This formula will help you say goodbye to goals and hello to results.

When we give up our goals to get results, we need to change how we think about results. We need to be results oriented. Take a moment and think about this. How results oriented are you? Do you always get the results you want? Do you even know what results you would like to achieve before the activity or do you just go? How you view results is often a barometer of how successful you are.

Why the RESULTS Formula? I found with my clients there were times that they were distracted and needed a way to keep focused. There were other clients who needed more accountability. Finally, there was a group of clients that kept asking me, "Am I normal?" and "Am I going to be ok?". The Formula can be used to ensure all of this and much more.

What is the RESULTS Formula? It is a seven-step process to follow that will improve your ability to get better results. In fact, I used the word RESULTS as an acronym to make it even easier to follow. HERE IT IS:

RESULTS FORMULA

R – Ready

E – End

S – Steps

U – You

L – Levels

T – Transform

S – Success

Let's examine each letter in detail, so you can better understand what The RESULTS Formula means and how you can implement it to achieve greater results. In later chapters, I will break down each letter, but for now, let me provide you an overview, so you have a basic understanding of the Formula.

R - READY

The "R" in The RESULTS Formula stands for "Ready." To achieve greater results, you need to be ready. Most people are not. In this book, I will discuss what it means to be ready and how you can ensure you are always ready to achieve the results you desire.

E - END

The "E" in The RESULTS Formula stands for "End." Once you are ready, you must think about what end result you want to achieve. What does the end result look like? The best way to achieve something is to visualize what outcome you want first. I even have a name for this type of thinking. It is called Z to A Results Thinking. I will explain more about this later in the book.

S - STEPS

After you have determined what you want to achieve, then you need to think about the steps required to achieve that result. The "S" in The RESULTS Formula stands for "Steps." A helpful hint is thinking about the steps as action steps. The more specific you make these actions steps, the more likely it is you will achieve the results you want.

U - YOU

The "U" in The RESULTS Formula stands for "You." I know I have taken a bit of license in that the first letter in the word "you" is a "y." However, in this day and age, so many people use the letter "u" to stand for the word "you". If others can do it then I thought I could use this substitute as well. Obviously to achieve greater results YOU need to be involved.

Being involved means you must work on yourself and your abilities. You need to work on the specific skills you need to achieve the results you desire. You need to continuingly work on your mindset, or what we call Caveman Brain®, as you become more successful and if you want to continue to achieve greater success.

This is an on-going process of investing in yourself so that you grow and be better tomorrow then you are today. However, once we graduate from school, many of us stop investing in ourselves. We stop learning. We don't pay the money to buy a book or go to a workshop or take a class or get a degree.

When you implement The RESULTS Formula, this non-investment thinking must stop. You will need to invest in yourself. I realize that you have started that process by reading this book, but I am going to tell you that you must go beyond just this book. Those who are truly successful NEVER stop learning because if they stop learning the stop growing.

The bottom line is if you are seeking greater outcomes, then you must invest in yourself in order to improve yourself. You have to be involved in every step, all the time. The RESULTS Formula takes commitment. That's why it works.

L - LEVELS

The "L" in The RESULTS Formula stands for "Levels of Learning." What do I mean by levels of learning? You are ready.

You thought about the end result you want to achieve. You have created and implementing specific action steps, and you are focusing on improving yourself. Now you are going to put your plan into action.

As you move through this process, you are going to start going through different levels of learning. Sometimes these levels go really fast. Other times they are going to take time. What happens as you pass through these levels is you are going to learn new skills, new knowledge, new habits, and new thought patterns.

Learning and growing personally and professionally are the keys to achieving results. There is just a word of caution about levels of learning: you may notice you are in a learning mode and you may not notice. It is really about how aware you are.

Many of us are looking for what I call the "big aha moments" that radically impact our learning. However, as we grow, those "aha moments" become less. Why? Levels of learning become about the little things, like a change of word that impacts our actions or a realignment of thought that opens the door to a new level of success.

In the beginning, gather all of the "big aha moments". As you continue on this journey, notice how the little changes you are making are impacting your outcomes. There are lots of examples of this in the levels of learning chapter later in the book.

T - TRANSFORMATION

The "T" in The RESULTS Formula stands for "Transformation." When we go through levels of learning, transformation will happen. We can't help but be transformed into a new way of thinking and a new way of being because of the learning we have experienced. Transformation means change.

I know there are so many people who are afraid of change. Let's face it, change is a part of life. I look at change and transformation as great things.

Remember the time when there were no cell phones, iPads or even computers? How about electricity? All of these things transformed our lives, and we were and are happy to have them! I am going to ask that you view change as positive.

If you are having a hard time with that thought, then I am going to ask you to question why? Are you afraid? Did you have a bad experience? It is often the negative thoughts we hear in our brains that will prevent us from moving forward.

If you want to achieve more, then know that transformation is a part of that. That means things are going to change. I could be like my mom who says, "build a bridge and get over it," but I know that when you have a fear of change, it can stop you in your path. I don't want that to happen to you.

I also don't want you to think that transformation is a bad thing. We all have transformed in one way or another. There can be positives as well as negatives to that experience.

When you think about transformation, I am going to ask you to stop looking for and acknowledging the negatives. I am going to ask that you start looking for and acknowledge the positives. Yes, I know the negatives are still there, but so are the positives. Positives, whether they are actions, words or thoughts move you forward. Negatives do not. When you embrace transformation, you will be able to move forward.

How will you know that you have transformed? You know you have transformed when you realize how you have changed from one point in time to another point in time. I'll expand on this concept in the transformation chapter.

S - SUCCESS

Transformation brings you to the last stage in The RESULTS Formula. The "S" in The RESULTS Formula stands for "Success." It takes hard work to achieve success. For almost all, achieving success is worth every step.

When you attain success, celebrate. Most people don't. Why is it important to celebrate? Our brains need a memorable reference point, also called a reward, to make the whole journey worthwhile! If we don't celebrate, everything just becomes a grind in life, and we become burned out.

When you celebrate the successes, you are giving your brain the feedback it needs to keep you moving toward new results. Therefore, I often expand success to include celebration. I call it "Success Celebrations". When you achieved success, then celebrate.

Now you know The RESULTS Formula.

The RESULTS Formula is a tool for my clients to use to help themselves to:

- Keep focused
- Be accountable
- Know that everything is alright

What is great about The RESULTS Formula is that it is repeatable. Once you achieve The RESULTS Formula, you can get yourself ready for the next level of success. When you are "ready" you can begin to implement The RESULTS Formula over and over again. You don't stop.

The rest of the book will break down each of the areas of The RESULTS Formula in specific details so you can give up your goals and say hello to results.

Now take the time to review what you learned. Write it down in the GET Results Now! Steps section. I know you may want to skip this exercise now so you can read the rest of the book, but I am going to encourage you to take just 5 minutes (or more), to do the exercise. This is how you are going to get more successful, by getting it out of your head and on a piece of paper. I find that when my clients write stuff down, it makes it real. Making it real, means that you can do something with it to make yourself more success.

👑 GET RESULTS NOW! STEPS

1. **Stop for a moment and think to yourself, "Am I ready to achieve greater results than what I have achieved in the past?" Write down your answer.**

   _____

   _____

   _____

   If you are read, turn the page…if not, keep going.

2. **If you are not ready, what is preventing you from being ready?**

    _____

    _____

3. **Do you think you can overcome this so you can be ready?**
    Y   N

If you are ready, move on to the next chapter. If you are not ready, then you need to think about what is stopping you and if you have a way to overcome those obstacles?

If you don't think you are ready to achieve more, then go back to the first exercise where you wrote down the results you want. See if the results you want to achieve will make you say yes. If the results don't make you say yes, then maybe the results aren't strong enough.

Results should be something you crave. If they are not strong enough or meaty enough for you to be ready to go get them, then they may not be truly the results you want. You may just have some goals that you need to get rid of and then start over again thinking about the results you want. This doesn't mean you did anything wrong; it just means you may need to dig deeper to define what result will get you off your butt and inspire you to achieve them.

CHAPTER 3

CAVEMAN BRAIN®

"A confused mind does nothing and
A stuck mind stays stuck."

Jean, The Results Queen®

Now you know The RESULTS formula. Before I start teaching you the in-depth steps of how to implement The RESULTS Formula into your life, I need to get your brain involved. I call this brain training. How and what do I mean by that? To help you achieve the results you desire, I want you to start training your brain.

Our brain is a very powerful tool. I want you to use this amazing tool to achieve greater results. Now there are many parts of our brain, but I am going to focus on one part, what I call our Caveman Brain®. That's what we all it in my training programs.

What is Caveman Brain? I'm sure you are all aware there was a time when we were cavemen, and of course, we had Caveman Brains. Part of our Caveman Brain is still with us today. It is at the bottom of the brain which means that it is at the base of your head.

There is a lot of research about our brain and the different parts. When I first started learning about brain training I thought it was a bunch of hyped-up junk, but now I realize I was wrong. In fact, I worked with a neuroscientist from Harvard University to learn more about brain training.

The research on developing and changing your neural pathways is amazing, and I recommend you read about this new area of study. However, I am going to make this simple for our purposes of being able to achieve the results we want. First, I call this part of our brain, Caveman Brain. Second, let me explain the way I see Caveman Brain and how I believe we can use it to achieve the results we want.

Back in our caveman days, there were a lot of dangerous things that could kill us. Part of the job of our Caveman Brain was to protect us. Think fight or flight or freeze. Our Caveman Brain constantly scanned the horizon – back and forth from left to right and right to left – for danger. If our brain heard or saw something, then the fight, flight or freeze instinct kicked in. This instinct holds true today.

Here is the problem. What was dangerous for us back in caveman times does not hold true for us in the modern world. There are no saber-tooth tigers hiding in the bushes waiting to pounce on us and kill us. However, Caveman Brain does not know that. It just knows it needs to protect us so we don't get killed.

Caveman Brain doesn't care if we are living in caveman times or modern times. It just knows to constantly scanning the horizon looking for danger. You can't stop it. You can't control it. What you can do is understand it and use it.

If there are no Saber-tooth tigers for our Caveman Brain to protect us from, what's a Caveman Brain to do? Our Caveman Brain looks for other "dangers." The problem is these other "dangers" may not be "dangers" at all. In fact, the Caveman Brain does not know reality from fiction.

Think about how you react when you watch a scary movie. You are watching as the killer is hiding around the corner and the victim is walking into the trap. What happens? Does your heart beat faster? Are you scared? Do you scream when the victim falls prey? How you react is all about Caveman Brain.

Your Caveman Brain is reacting to what it is hearing and what it seeing. You can't control the reaction. The reason is that your Caveman Brain does not separate reality from fiction. It just reacts to what it sees and what it hears. Your Caveman Brain is trying to protect you by telling you there is danger based on your senses. In the case of the scary movie, there is no real danger, yet our brains think there is and make our bodies act accordingly. Hence, we jump, gasp, and scream.

How does this apply to achieving greater results? Our Caveman Brain perceives dangers all around us, all the time. As our Caveman Brains scans for danger, it is always coming up with all types of things it considers "dangerous." It is up to us to decide if these "dangers" are dangerous enough for us to take flight, fight or freeze. In many cases, the "dangers" that our Caveman Brain is telling us about make us act in ways that may not be helpful for us or as I like to say, serve us well.

What are these "dangers"? That depends on the person. Let me give you an example. One day my son asked my mom what I did I do for a living. My mom said, "Your mother talks to strangers." Do you think talking to strangers is dangerous? For me no. For you, maybe or even yes. If it is a yes, then talking to strangers is a "danger" for you.

Here is another "danger" I get a lot from my clients. Public speaking. I can't tell you how many clients come to me telling me how fearful they are about speaking in public. For them, public speaking is a "danger".

If you are not aware that these "dangers" are not dangers at all, then these "dangers" can prevent you from getting to your endgame and the end results that you desire. These "dangers" will often hold us back and prevent us from moving toward something we really want.

For us to achieve more results, we have to eliminate or at least minimize the "dangers" that are holding us back. In other words, we have to get the Caveman Brain to work with us and not against us. Let me give you an example of what I mean.

Have you ever heard a voice inside your head? I know it sounds crazy, but go with me on this. There is a voice inside of your head, and it constantly speaks to you. It may say, "Wow, great job." This voice also says, "You suck." "Why did you do that?" "You are so stupid." You get the picture. This voice is our Caveman Brain speaking to us.

You probably never really focused on that voice. It just has been with you...forever. That voice is your Caveman Brain doing its best to protect you. That's the reason why it is often negative. It is the only way that it knows how to protect you. This inner voice is part of your Caveman Brain's system to get you to take flight, fight or freeze.

Usually, our inner voice does not say a lot of positive things to us. If it is not always positive what happens? Remember when I said earlier the brain only reacts to what it sees and what it hears? Well, it responses to your inner voice too. If your inner voice is negative, image how that is working for you...it's not! It is working against you.

Now that you know that voice is a negative voice because it's your Caveman Brain trying to protect you, what can we do to focus that voice on helping us? We can't eliminate this voice, but we can use it to our advantage. Now I am sure you are asking yourself, "Jean, if Caveman Brain is constantly scanning for danger, how do we use that to our advantage?"

The first step in harnessing your Caveman Brain is knowing that the Caveman Brain is going to be negative. This is important because every time you hear that negative voice in your head then you know that is your Caveman Brain talking.

I am going to ask you to be aware of those negative thoughts that are being played inside your head. Awareness is half the battle. Many of us don't even hear these negative thoughts. Remember when I said that your brain acts on what it sees and what it hears?

If your Caveman Brain keeps hearing negative thoughts, what do you think it is going to do? Your Caveman Brain is going to try to protect you. Remember that's Caveman Brain's job! Yet, if there is nothing to be protected from then can you see how your Caveman Brain can stop you?

The next step in harnessing your Caveman Brain is figuring out how to change these negative thoughts into positive ones. To do this, you need to thank your Caveman Brain for protecting you. Yes, you can read that line again. You need to thank your Caveman Brain for protecting you. Before I lose you, let me explain.

What I have found for my clients and myself is, if I say out loud, "Thank you Caveman Brain for protecting me," the negative thought tends to go away. It really goes away when I complete the sentence with something positive: "Thank you Caveman Brain for protecting me, and I am going to . . . " When I redirect my Caveman Brain to a positive thought, my brain tends to focus on the positive and forgets about the negative. Let me give you an example.

I have a client who asked me how to get more prospects into his sales funnel. I suggested he host an executive breakfast. While I won't go into lots of details about an executive breakfast, I will say this. An executive breakfast is when you host a breakfast either in your offices or a hotel, and you invite eight to ten people. Two of those eight to ten people are current clients who LOVE you. The others are prospects. It is a way to get a bunch of prospects into your funnel quickly.

When I suggested this idea to my client, without any hesitation, the first words out of his mouth were, "I can't do that. No one will come." "Really?" I asked, "No one will come? Not even the two clients who LOVE you?" My client thought about it and then said, "Yes, you are right. My two clients who love me would come."

Notice my client's first reaction to my idea: "I can't do that. No one will come." This response is Caveman Brain at work. My client's first reaction was negative. The "no one will come" statement is a caveman reaction. Do you think no one will come to my client's executive breakfast? Not even the two clients who love this person?

When I asked the above line of questioning to my client, he said, "Well, of course, my two clients who love me will come." When I asked him what made him state, very empathically, "no one will come," he told me it was just his first reaction. Notice it was his first reaction. It was a negative reaction. It was Caveman Brain at work.

Once we had discussed the topic more fully, he realized, of course, his clients would attend his meeting. He believed he could get his two clients to bring along two prospects and he believed he could get another four prospects to attend the breakfast. The initial "no way" reaction went to a "yes, hosting an executive breakfast would be a good thing for my business."

Can you see the power of the Caveman Brain? Think about my client's first reaction. What was it about? What happens when "no one will come?" Can you see how this one sentence shows how Caveman Brain works? Can you see how Caveman Brain is working to protect us? If not, let me give you the running dialogue from the Caveman Brain point of view, so you understand how the Caveman Brain is working hard to protect you.

I want you to read the next paragraph as you think a Caveman would. You don't need to read it out loud. Just listen to your brain as you read the paragraph.

Caveman Brain wouldn't want you to have an event where no one would show up. What could happen to you if no one was there? You would be alone which is bad because if you are alone, then you could get killed. It is better not to go there by yourself. Also, if no one comes, then that could mean people are rejecting you. Who wants to suffer rejection?

Here are some more thoughts. No one coming could mean it won't work. It could be a waste of time and money. It could be scary. Why? Maybe no one coming highlights that no one likes you. No one believes in you. That having this job is not good for you. You can't be successful in this job.

It could cause embarrassment. No one came. How do you explain that? What does that mean? How will you be judged? Wouldn't people think you are a loser because you can't get people to come to your event? Maybe you aren't good at making friends or connections. Hosting an executive breakfast would show to you and the world that you have no friends. I don't want to highlight that you have no friends because that would mean you are alone. Being alone means we could be killed.

This list could go on. You get the picture now, don't you? Isn't it easier not to do this because of any and all of the above?

Did any of these thoughts cross your mind as you read the initial story about my client? If they did, then you too experienced Caveman Brain. Can you see how these thoughts can stop you from moving forward? Do you see how these thoughts can stop you from getting to the end result you want?

What if I hadn't helped my client through that situation? Do you think he would have gone through with the executive breakfast or just given up the idea and moved on to the next? Do you think he could have found anything that would have helped him fill his sales funnel quickly or do you think he would have just stayed stuck, trying to figure out what to do next?

How many times do we just stand still stuck? Often we are stuck because our Caveman Brain has frozen. Remember flight, fight or freeze. When you are "frozen," start exploring your thoughts. It could be your thoughts that are stopping you from moving forward.

Let me point out some more things your Caveman Brain may have said to you that could be stopping you from going forward. Check off the ones that apply to you. Note, it could be all of them. One more point: Be honest with yourself. No one is looking at these but you. If you are not honest now, then how will you successfully move forward?

Here are some caveman thoughts my clients have experienced. Check off the ones that apply to you. Oh, and feel free to add to the list as well. This is just a partial list. You know there are always more.

♛ CAVEMAN BRAIN® THOUGHTS

____ I am not good enough, so there is no reason to try.

____ _____is always going to be better than me, so what's the point?

____ I can't go to that networking group because I won't know anyone.

____ I can't make that call because they will say no.

____ I don't know what to say.

____ These things never work.

Now do you understand how Caveman Brain works? This is the running dialogue in your head. I am sure when I told my client that idea, those thoughts I just mentioned or thoughts just like those, immediately popped into his head. Remember, his first reaction was he couldn't do it. Maybe when you read his story, you had the same thoughts.

I'm always amazed at how quickly Caveman Brain operates. Of course it has to operate at lightning speed. It has to protect you. It is always protecting you.

So how do we direct the power of our Caveman Brain to help us rather than hold us back? First, we need to thank our Caveman Brain. Second, we tell Caveman Brain what we are going to do instead using positive language. This is how we direct the power of our Caveman Brain.

When we acknowledge the negative thought, then Caveman Brain knows it has done its job. By introducing the new thought, we are letting our Caveman Brain know this new thought is ok and not something we need protection from.

What we are telling Our Caveman Brain is that this new thought needs our Caveman Brain's support. What I find really interesting is when you say that new thought to your Caveman Brain, your Caveman Brain says, "Fine, I can do that." It is that simple. It is always not that easy because you have to be aware and do this exercise each and every time to redirect your Caveman Brain to support you in what you want to do.

Your Caveman Brain wants to protect you. It wants to make sure that you survive. It doesn't know positive or negative. It knows dead or not dead. This means you can train your brain to help you achieve more results. How? We need to feed our Caveman Brain positive thoughts. To feed your Caveman Brain positive thoughts, try this:

"Thank you, Caveman Brain, for protecting me by telling me (the negative statement). However, everything is going to be ok, and I choose (the positive statement)."

Whatever your inner voice tells you, reverse it and say the positive. Now at this point, my clients will say, "what if I don't believe the new positive statement?" This is another area where we can implement brain training. Remember our brains react to what they hear and what they see. If you start saying positive statements rather than negative, your brain will believe it.

Let me give you an example. When you buy a new car, how often do you see that car? You see it everywhere. The reason is your brain wants to reinforce to you that you did the right thing. When you take an action, your brain does its best to reinforce that you did the right thing. I believe it is part of the survival instinct.

When you accept the negative statements your inner voice says to you, your brain does its best to find things to reinforce it for you. When you start to accept the positive sayings, your brain will look for positive reinforcements even if you don't believe it.

Another thing, if you say these positive statements over and over again, the brain will believe these new positive statements. This is part of brain training. Saying the positive statement two times a day for thirty days will pretty much kill the negative statement. If a negative statement raises its ugly head from time to time, follow the steps above, and stop it before the negative statement can ever take root.

A way to monitor your negative statements is to start keeping a list or a journal of what your inner voice is saying to you and when it is saying it. Keeping a record will make you aware of what is going on with your inner voice. Once you record the negative statement, write down the positive statement. Say that positive statement two times a day for the next 30 days. I like to say that statement or statements, yes there can be more than one, when I first get up in the morning and when I go to bed at night.

This process will help you transition those negative statements into positive ones. Don't worry if you have a long list of statements to read. When I did this process, there was a time when I had a page of statements I read every day. Image a whole page!

Again, when you hear that inner voice speak negatively to you, write it down. Then write out the positive statement. Say that positive statement two times a day for 30 days, and that negative thought will disappear.

I am telling you this because everything that I have written in this book, I have done myself. Once I have proved that it works for me, then I use the techniques with my clients. I don't ever want to make my clients do things that I know won't work. The stakes are too high!

Harnessing your Caveman Brain takes vigilance. It is something you must constantly be aware of and correct immediately. It is a simple process. It is not always an easy process.

Harnessing your Caveman Brain takes commitment. You need to be willing to refocus your Caveman Brain and commit to the effort, every minute, every hour, every day, every week and every year. I am telling you that you have to make a choice to do this. You have to commit. If you don't refocus your Caveman Brain, then it will always stop you from the greatness you are meant to achieve.

Remember your Caveman Brian is constantly scanning the horizon for danger. That means your Caveman Brain is constantly feeding your subconscious and your conscious those thoughts that will keep you alive. Those thoughts are not always positive. It is up to you to take the thoughts that are not helpful and make them helpful so you can be even more successful. How can you do that? Here is a process you can use to refocus those thoughts that are not helpful to thoughts that will propel you.

CAVEMAN BRAIN® MANAGEMENT PROCESS

1. I am committed to refocusing my Caveman Brain to help me achieve the results I want.
2. I know that my Caveman Brain is always protecting me.
3. I can recognize my Caveman Brain because it tells me negative thoughts. I acknowledge that my Caveman Brain is working to protect me.
4. I understand I need to reverse the negative thoughts to positive ones.
5. I am aware of what my Caveman Brain is saying because I am monitoring my inner voice.

Every time I hear my Caveman Brain say something negative to me, I say "Thank you Caveman Brain for protecting me." Saying it out loud helps to calm my Caveman Brain even more.

I do that by saying the positive statement out loud because my brain only reacts to what it sees and what it hears. By saying the positive statement out loud, my brain hears it and responses.

Once you have successfully gone through these steps, you are on your way to harnessing your Caveman Brain. You will have to repeat this process over and over again until all of the negative statements are gone, and your brain provides you with positive statements. Of course, since your Caveman Brain is there to protect you, it will constantly and consistently come up with "dangers." However, you now have the process to address those "dangers" when they arise so you can get to the end and obtain the results you want.

The final step in harnessing your Caveman Brain is probably the most powerful. Remember the example of the scary movie? Caveman Brain only understands what it sees and what it hears, whether or not it is a reality. So how do we use this part of our Caveman Brain that reacts to what it sees and what it hears? We need to change what we are feeding our brains. What are your feeding yours?

Think about it this way. If you are always hearing or seeing negative stuff, what do you think your reactions are? Of course, negative. Let me give you an example.

One late night I decided to watch *The Piano*. This is an old movie I had never seen but had heard about when I was a kid. While not a scary movie, I did find it very upsetting for a variety of reasons. For almost three days after I watched this movie, I didn't feel right. Not that I was ill. I just was depressed and couldn't get myself motivated.

I started to review what could have made me feel this way, and the only thing that was different in my routine was the late night movie. I stopped watching late night movies, and I also started only watching movies I knew I could feel good about.

In fact, I went on a negative diet and started eliminating all negativity from my life. That included the nightly news and specific people. Once you get rid of the negative energy, you will be amazed at how positive things can become

I would suggest you try this experiment. Go on a negative diet. See what negative forces are in your life.

What are you watching on TV? What movies are you watching? What video games are you playing? When you are having conversations with other people are you focusing on the negative or the positive? Are you hanging out with the wrong people? Do these people make you feel good or bad when you hang out with them?

Let me give you another story that I think will highlight the negative diet and what to do. I had a long time colleague that I didn't see that often but when I did we always had a ton of fun. We would discuss different people and situations that were going on in our lives. I never realized how negative these conversation were until one day another colleague who happened to be with us said to me, "Jean, I never knew how negative you were." Boy was that awake up call. I gradually stopped seeing this colleague and started going to other conferences where I could meet new colleagues and now people say to me, "Jean, how can you be so positive all the time?" If I can do it, you can to.

I can hear you saying, "what if a negative energy in my life is a family member? I can't eliminate them." No, you can't. However, you don't have to take on their negativity.

When your relative is negative, and your Caveman Brain agrees, first thank your Caveman Brain for protecting you and then say, "that is about them, it is not about me." Keep saying that statement and it will help. It won't change your negative relative. It will change you.

Caveman Brain is always going to be with you. Now that you know, that you can focus your Caveman Brain on helping you achieve the results you want.

♛ GET RESULTS NOW! STEPS

1. What negative things are you saying to yourself right now? Write them down and then write out the positive statements. Say these positive statements twice a day for 30 days and watch those negative thoughts go away.

   _____

   _____

   _____

2. What activities are you doing right now that are having a negative impact on you? Write them down and eliminate them.

   _____

   _____

   _____

3. Continue to monitor your thoughts and your actions. Make sure you are constantly focused on the positive and not the negative.

   _____

   _____

   _____

4. Make sure to thank your Caveman Brain.

   _____

   _____

   _____

5. If you need more space for this exercise then here you go.

_____

_____

_____

_____

_____

_____

_____

_____

_____

_____

_____

_____

_____

_____

_____

_____

_____

_____

_____

_____

CHAPTER 4

GET COMFORTABLE BEING UNCOMFORTABLE

"Build a bridge and get over it."

Jean, The Results Queen®

Most of us don't like being uncomfortable. In fact, for many of us, we seek out comfort. We like our comfort food. We like sleeping in our comfortable beds. We don't like things that make us feel uncomfortable.

The problem is that learning happens when we are uncomfortable. If we don't like being uncomfortable, what happens? We stop learning. If we are not learning, then we are not growing.

How do most of us learn? While many of us learn on the job or what has been called just-in-time learning, the majority of us learn by reading. In fact, 80 percent of us are visual learners, meaning we learn by reading. While ten percent of us learn by doing, also called kinesthetic learning, the remaining five percent learn by listening. Learning by listening is called auditory learning. If the majority of us learn by reading, what happens if we stop reading?

According to a survey conducted by the Jenkins group in 2003:
- One-third of high school graduates never read another book for the rest of their lives.
- 42 percent of college graduates never read another book after college.

- 80 percent of U.S. families did not buy or read a book last year.
- 70 percent of U.S. adults have not been in a bookstore in the last five years.
- 57 percent of new books are not read to completion.

I find this sad because books, articles, magazines, blogs, and news sources are several areas that can provide ideas and stimulate conversation allowing us to grow and be better tomorrow than we are today. If we can't find ideas to expand our horizons, how can we achieve the results we want?

It is important to always be learning because when you stop learning, you stop growing. I have a colleague that ensures she keeps learning by attending an offsite conference every month. She says that getting out of the office and attending workshops provides her the insights and information needed for her to continue to run her company successfully.

I know you are reading this book to help you grow. There are also other ways you can grow: Hire a coach, join a mastermind group, and/or read a book every two weeks. To keep growing, you must keep pushing yourself out of your comfort zone.

I recently read that Warren Buffet, one of the wealthiest men in the world, reads a book a day. Maybe that is his secret. I also think, a book a day? That's a lot of reading, but again, maybe that is his secret. In any event, if you can increase your reading, I believe you will increase your success.

I read a lot. People often ask me what I read. I always read Harvard Business Review (HBR). HBR provides lots of articles on business. I read the "Corner Office" in The Sunday New York Times. I am usually reading several books at once. Believe it or not, I read on my cell phone. If the book is really hard to read on that device, then I will buy it in hardcover. I like to highlight and bend corners.

I had a colleague who read the same five books every year. He would just read them over and over, year after year. He said he always learned something new. I would agree with reading things over again because when you read it a second time, you often find new things to work on. The reason I am telling you to start reading or to read more is because reading may be an activity that is right now out of your comfort zone.

Let's talk about coaches. Since I started my business, I have always had a coach. Some I have been with for a short time, others I have been with for years. Sometimes I have had one coach, and there are other times I have had up to four at once. I have learned from my coaches using them as sounding boards, strategic partners, or someone to hold me accountable.

There were times that I could only pay the coach and I couldn't pay myself. I always paid the coach before I paid myself and during those times lived out of my comfort zone to make it work. I believe in coaching. I live to learn one-on-one. This is another activity that you may want to engage in because it will force you to get out of your comfort zone.

There are others who learn better in a group setting. For those people, try group coaching. Group coaching can be very beneficial because you can hear many different points of view and learn from them.

No matter what, please find ways to continue to learn because that is how you will grow and be more successful. If you find you need both individual coaching and the dynamics of a group setting, that's ok – do them both. Remember learning is pushing yourself out of your comfort zone. If you are not learning, then you are dying.

There are some folks that don't believe in coaching. I think the reason why is that it makes them feel uncomfortable or they just don't think they need it. They think the can do everything by themselves. However, we don't always learn by ourselves. We learn faster when we have others around us. I only hope those people who feel this way are using other learning formats to grow.

Other learning formats could be going to monthly workshops and/or conferences, having a mastermind group, a mentor, or an accountability partner. You may feel uncomfortable participating in any or all for a variety of reasons which, could include time, money or how do I do this. What I am going to say is build a bridge and get over it. When you are uncomfortable you are learning. When you are learning, you are growing and when you are growing, you are more successful. Who doesn't want to be more successful?

Allow me to clarify one thing for those who don't know what an accountability partner is, it is one person you speak to that holds you accountable. An accountability partner can come from anywhere. My first accountability partner I met at a workshop. Others have come from different groups that I participate in. It doesn't matter how you find an accountability partner. It matters that you find one.

The whole point is to have someone you can speak to once a week that you tell what you will accomplish and they will hold you to that. You can speak daily or weekly. Longer than that and I don't think it works.

On the call, each person takes a turn to tell the other what they will accomplish. On the next call, you report what you accomplished and what you will accomplish in the next time period. When you have someone holding you accountable, you will be amazed at what you get done!

Here is another place where being uncomfortable taught me a lot, I had one coach who once told me the way you run one mile is the way you do business. I have given that a lot of thought and concluded she is right. How do I know that? Well, I started running, and I'm going to share with you what I have learned.

Now to be up front, I hate running. It is way out of my comfort zone and to me, there is nothing about I consider fun. With that said, running is how I learned how to get comfortable being uncomfortable.

There are lots of mornings I want to stay in bed and not exercise at all. Guess what I do? To be totally transparent, I just say to myself, "Nope, not today." I stay in my comfort zone. Does that help me grow? No, it doesn't.

In fact, what usually happens is many hours after I have made this decision of indulging my comfort zone, I think "Heck, why didn't I get up and run? I could have!" I start kicking myself because I missed a learning opportunity and I did that to myself! Remember growing happens when you are outside of your comfort zone. Since Caveman Brain doesn't want us to get out of our comfort zone, we often self-sabotage ourselves so that we stay within our comfort zone.

Self-sabotaging is a way of staying in your comfort zone. There is a reason why I am telling you this. The reason is if we aren't careful we can self-sabotage ourselves all the time. Many times we self-sabotage ourselves without ever realizing we are doing it. Again, we do this so we can stay in our comfort zone. It is only upon reflection we regret the choices we made. For some of us, we don't even take the time to reflect; we just keep self-sabotaging ourselves. It is important to know when you are self-sabotaging yourself because it is often means you are staying in your comfort zone, when you need to break out and be uncomfortable.

I've already told you I can't stand running. However, I keep running. Why? I run because I know how much I learn from this activity. Running consistently keeps me out of my comfort zone. Remember when you are out of your comfort zone you are learning.

Running also makes me stronger. It helps me build stamina, and since I don't listen to anything when I run, but the sound of the great outdoors, it provides me with clarity time. What's clarity time? That's the time I take to get really clear on the results I want to achieve. If you don't make clarity time, I would strongly urge you to start. If you are not clear about what results you want, how will you ever get the results you want? Additionally, if you want to be able to achieve the results you want, you need to have the strength and the stamina to get that result.

If you are not fit enough to hold yourself up, how can you run the race it will take to achieve the result you desire? You must learn to live outside of your comfort zone every single day. It is important to know when you are in your comfort zone, when you are stuck in your comfort zone and when you need to get out of your comfort zone. It is also important to know when you are comfortable being uncomfortable. A coach, a mastermind group, and/or an accountability partner can help you keep on track with this method because they can reflect back to you what stage you are in.

Everyone has their comfort zone. What is great is about this is that you can team up with others to help you live outside of your comfort zone. Let me give you an example. I am in a mastermind group where we discussed our running styles. One of my colleagues has learned she starts strong and often gets distracted at the end. I have another colleague who starts off too fast, loses steam in the middle and finishes strong at the end. For me, I hate starting, but once I get started, I always finish. Knowing this about ourselves and each other allows us to help each. My mastermind group helps me get started. I can help my colleagues stay on track or finish the project because I know where she is likely to fall back into her comfort zone.

How do these lessons translate into results? Let's say you were assigned a project. If you are like my first colleague, you will start the project off strong, but you may never get it completed because you fade at the end. If you are like my second colleague, you will just start the project without giving it a bit of thought. You will think, "I got to start this fast." However, you might find that without some preplanning, things won't go so well in the end. If you are like me, you will take some time to get started, but once you do, there will be no stopping you.

Let me give you another example. One of my sales coaches runs and told me what she has learned from the sport; she starts out strong and finishes weak. As in the sport, so it is in life. When it comes time to start the sales process, she always has in mind the number of sales she wants. In other words, she knows the results she wants to achieve. She has a strong process for getting and closing clients. However, she tells me that while she starts off strong, there are times she falls short of her sales results because she wasn't finishing strong. How did she realize she wasn't finishing strong? From running. When she is running, she always starts out strong and finishes weak. Now that she knows that about herself, she applies specific techniques to ensure that it doesn't happen to her when she is selling. She knows when she is in her comfort zone and when she is not and adjusts accordingly either on her own or with the help of those she has surrounded herself with…her coach, her mastermind group and her accountability partner.

When it comes to being in or out of your comfort zone, here is an important point to remember: How you do one thing is how you do everything. That is why running is so important because how I run, is how I do everything else. I tell this to my clients all the time.

When you start realizing what actions you are doing, where you are implementing these actions and in the way you are implementing them, you can start to change these actions to get the results you want. You can stop self-sabotaging and get comfortable being uncomfortable.

I can bet you that your current actions are not helping you achieve the results you want. It is only after you have identified and changed these actions you will achieve your desired results. Again, this means start being comfortable being under comfortable…today.

Here is another thing you need to know about this process. It is ongoing. Just keep thinking "how you do one thing is how you do everything." If you want things to continually change, you need to continually change the things that are not helping you achieve the results you want. I have learned to live everyday in my uncomfortable zone. I know when I slide out of my uncomfortable zone and back into my comfort zone. I know how to get out of my comfort zone back into my space of comfortableness. There is a reason why I know this.

The reason is that I know I know no matter what happens, there will be times when I go back into my comfort zone. Hey I am human too. I know that this is a journey. When you are on a journey there are times when you are going to fall down. It is how you get up and back on track that matters.

It is also important to figure out what is in your comfort zone and what is out of it. I spent a whole year working on being uncomfortable all of the time. Why? I want to ensure I am growing and I believe if I stay firmly planted in my comfort zone I won't grow. This is one of the main reasons I took up running. I am suggesting you do too or something like running.

I know some of you are going to say, "Jean, I can't run due to a physical injury." Ok. Then what are you going to do to get out of your comfort zone? When you are willing to push yourself out of your comfort zone, and you have the ability to get comfortable being uncomfortable you will grow. My girlfriend can't run so she took up working out. It is what makes her uncomfortable.

What's stopping you?

Let's talk about food. Food is an area that is very easy for us to be in our comfort zone and indulge in self-sabotage. We eat without thinking, and later we think, "Why the heck did I eat that?"

Awhile back I was at a conference where snacks were served in the afternoon. You know the type of snacks I am talking about, right? Cookies, brownies, candy with soda, coffee, and tea. I passed. The next morning, another participant came up to me and said, "I noticed you didn't have any snacks yesterday." This person told me that he did have the snacks and then later thought, "Why wasn't I like Jean and not have any snacks? I really didn't need that." This person said he decided that today he wasn't going to have snacks. He said, "I am going to be like Jean and pass on the snacks."

Believe it or not, that is living out of your comfort zone. It is doing something that few others will do. What I also realized from the conversation was while you don't need the snacks, you also never know who is watching you!

Here is my last story of living outside of your comfort zone. My daughter is a competitive equestrian. In all the years she has been riding, I have only read two books about horses and horseback riding. I also can only remember one fact from each book. I am going to share one of those facts because it is about being uncomfortable. I still think about it and talk about it today. Here it is: Horses and humans share something in common. Apparently, both horses and humans are born lazy. There is nothing a horse would rather do than lie around and eat all day. It is only when a horse is made to do something, they actually do something. Hmmm. Being lazy is another way we stay in our comfort zone.

The reason I tell you this one horse fact is as I said before I use it. I often repeat this to myself when I am lying in bed not wanting to exercise. I have to make myself do something, or no action happens, and most of the time if I truly want something to happen, I have to be out of my comfort zone.

The RESULTS Formula is going to make you feel uncomfortable. I want you to be prepared for it because if not, you may not continue to use it. Remember getting comfortable being uncomfortable is a skill and a very valuable one. It is truly only those who remain in the uncomfortable zone that are successful.

♛ GET RESULTS NOW! STEPS

1. Describe your comfort zone.

_____

_____

_____

2. Describe what you feel like when you are in your comfort zone

_____

_____

_____

3. What makes you uncomfortable?

_____

_____

_____

4. If you learned to do the thing(s) that made you uncomfortable would you achieve the results you want? Yes or No

5. Are you willing to take up running?   Yes or No
   Why or why not?

_____

_____

_____

6. **If not, what activity are you willing to take up to assist you in getting out of your comfort zone?**

    - Swimming
    - Walking
    - Biking
    - Speaking in public

    - Writing a book
    - Going to a networking group
    - Volunteering at a workshop
    - Other activities

7. **How will you know you are out of your comfort zone?**

    _____

    _____

    _____

8. **If you stayed out of your comfort zone, would you be more successful?**

    _____

    _____

    _____

CHAPTER 5

OTHER PEOPLE'S BAGGAGE

*"At some point, it all becomes about
managing your mindset to achieve results."*

Jean, The Results Queen®

What do I mean by Other People's Baggage? Other People's Baggage refers to the stories we tell ourselves each day that our not our stories. They are the stories that have come from our childhood, our culture, our experiences and our parents. These are the stories we have learned and have made a part of our lives. These are stories that have helped us throughout our lives. However, now these stories may no longer be serving us in terms of what we want to achieve.

We have to identify these stories so we can get rid of them and replace them with the stories that will help you get to the level of success. I am going to talk about more about this later in the chapter because before I go on about what I call OPB (other people's luggage), and now that you understand the importance of living in your uncomfortable zone, we need to develop your Results Mindset.

Remember Caveman Brain? Your Caveman Brain plays a big role in building your Results Mindset. Remember how I told you always to thank your Caveman Brain? I hope you have been practicing because now it is time to start managing your Caveman Brain so you can develop your Results Mindset.

What do I mean when I say Results Mindset? When you are at the top of your game, it is no longer about your skill set. It becomes about your mindset. It becomes about managing the your Results mindset.

Now I want to be clear. You can only start working on developing your Results Mindset if you have gotten control of your Caveman Brain and you are comfortable being uncomfortable. If you have those two things down, the Results Mindset is within your reach.

Your Results Mindset starts with Your Inner Voice

What is your inner voice? I know this may sound crazy, so bear with me, I believe we all have an inner voice. The inner voice is the voice inside your brain that is always telling you what you did wrong. "Why did you say that?" The inner voice is the voice in your brain that says, "You should have said this."

As you become more successful, this inner voice grows louder and more critical. You have to learn how to quiet this inner voice. Notice I didn't say eliminate the inner voice. I don't think you can eliminate that inner voice. Why? You still are going to need your Caveman Brain to protect you from those things that could actually hurt you.

When you learn to quiet the inner voice, it will support your efforts to become more successful. You must be aware of this so you can purposefully manage it. I find this is the biggest challenge for my clients because it is the last obstacle that often holds them back from truly achieving success. They don't consistently manage their mindset.

That inner voice is constantly running all day long, and it only has negative things to say. Why only negative things? Remember the inner voice is part of the Caveman Brain's system to ensure that you are always protected.

Since the inner voice is part of the system that is trying to protect us, of course, it is only going to highlight the things that can harm us. Translation . . . usually the negative stuff in life. Remember Caveman Brain only believes what it hears and what it sees. It doesn't know reality from fiction. It looks at everything as can it hurt us or not.

I find a lot of the negative thoughts people have almost always start with a "don't." Things like:
- Don't go there
- Don't talk to strangers
- Don't touch that
- Don't make a fool of yourself

Now think about how many don'ts you have in your life. I bet you have a lot of them. Why do you have so many of them? I think the reason is that our parents wanted to keep us safe. Guess what is at work to keep us safe? Caveman Brain. Many of our adult "don'ts" have been past down from our childhood, our parents, our live experiences and our culture.

The challenge is as adults we don't review these stories. They are just part of our lives. Unfortunately, these stories often based on how we were raised as children and the Caveman Brain of our parents. If you are in charge of a child, think of what you say to protect the child. That is why we have so many don'ts in our lives. It is the Caveman Brain working on protecting us and those of people in our lives. If you don't believe me, go back and look at the list. Most of those things were said to protect us. These sayings come from other people's Caveman Brains because they are trying to protect themselves and those around them.

I am going to keep reminding you that Caveman Brain is here to protect you. The reason? I often find from working with my clients is that OPB is what is holding them back from being more successful. It is these "don'ts" that are holding them back.

Think for a minute about all the don'ts you were taught and how they followed you through life. When you were little, your parents admonished you "don't speak to strangers." Now in your job, how many "strangers" do you meet? Most of us are required to meet strangers all the time. When were you told it was ok to speak to strangers?

In fact, my son once asked my mom what did I do for a living. My mom told him that my job is to talk to strangers. It started making me think, when did I get permission to do that?

As children, we are constantly told to avoid dangerous things. Unfortunately, no one ever gives us permission to stop doing these dangerous things. We just start doing them because the danger is not as great for adults as it is for children. These stories become our baggage. Yet, it is not our baggage. It is other people's baggage. That is why we need to get rid of it. This baggage is not yours. You didn't create it. Someone else did. Their baggage became your baggage. Often OPB is what is holding you back.

Here's the problem. We still carry all of that "don't baggage" from when we were kids, along with a lot of other baggage we often don't address as adults. This baggage can and does often hinder our growth and success later in life. Only when we decide to eliminate this baggage can we clear those obstacles preventing us from achieving that next level we so crave.

One of my coaches, Alan Weiss, used to say, "Throw your old baggage off the train and create your own baggage." He was right because the baggage we carry around is often someone else's baggage. Wouldn't it be great if you could just deal with your stuff rather than the stuff your mom, dad, family, friends, and teachers told you about all day? That is what Alan meant when he said to throw your baggage off the train because it's not yours. I don't know about you, but I don't want to carry anyone else's baggage around . . . do you?

Let me give you an example. I had a client whose dad expected her to be the smartest person in the room. When she brought home a 98 on her test, he wouldn't celebrate the 98; he would ask, "What happened to the other two points?" He expected her to get 100% on everything. Talk about an impossible feat for a child, right? Do you think you could get 100% on every single thing, every single day?

Now think about how this pressure translates for this woman as an adult. When was the last time you were perfect every time you did something? When we learn something new, few of us do it perfectly, yet this woman expected she should always get everything right. She was frustrated it took her so long to accomplish new things. After she had thrown her dad's "baggage from the train," her accomplishments became easier and more enjoyable. She was learning and doing on her terms, not her dad's terms.

Here is another example. A very close friend of mine was told by his dad that "he peaked at two." He was told this one sentence over and over again for more than 30 years. Can you imagine your whole life thinking you peaked at two? How would you act? What would you say about yourself? If you live 80 years, how the heck do you peak at two?

Guess whose baggage that was? That baggage belonged to my friend's dad, but my friend carried it around. However, once my friend worked through this baggage, he decided it was time to get rid of it. He decided he hadn't peaked yet and he wanted the rest of his life back so he could peak when he decided he wanted to. That's throwing baggage off the train!

These two examples show how we pick up other people's points of view and let them affect our lives. As I said before, Alan Weiss has it right. We need to identify other people's points of view we use to view ourselves. Once identified, we need to work on getting rid of them if we find they are not working for us.

Sometimes that is easier said than done especially when we try to do this by ourselves. If you are ready to get rid of this baggage and you can't do it by yourself, I would suggest getting an outsider to help you work through this. It could be a friend, a therapist, a coach, and/or a religious leader. Why do I say this? Based on my experience, I find it may take more than one person to help you eliminate this baggage.

Many of my clients tell me they hire me to help them in business and they have a second person to help them with their personal lives. I know people who start with a therapist and then hire a business coach. I know other people who do the opposite. One thing I have observed is when you are working on all aspects of getting rid of your baggage, both in your personal and business life, you are ready to achieve amazing things.

♛ GET RESULTS NOW! STEPS

1. **Write a list of all of the "Don'ts" you tell yourself.**

_____

_____

_____

_____

_____

_____

_____

_____

_____

_____

_____

_____

_____

2. Take your "Don't" list and change it into a "Can Do" list.

_____

_____

_____

_____

_____

_____

_____

_____

_____

_____

_____

_____

_____

_____

3. Review your list twice every day to make sure you are eliminating those things on your don't list. I would suggest reviewing it once in the morning and once before you go to bed.

CHAPTER 6

RESULTS MINDSET

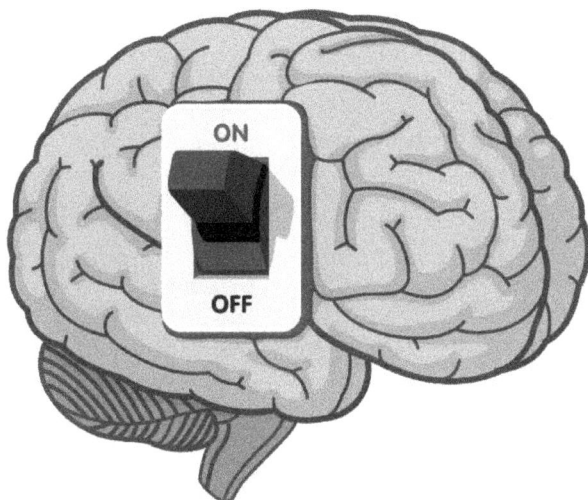

*"When your mindset is set to results,
results is what you get."*

Jean, The Results Queen®

There comes a point when achieving greater success is not about skill set. It becomes about mindset. How will you know when you get to this point?

You will know you have entered the mindset game where it is no longer about skill set when you keep going to all of those workshops, you read all of those books, you pay for all of those classes and programs, and you are not achieving the results you want. I call this looking for the silver bullet.

What is the silver bullet? If you look up the definition, you will find that a silver bullet is defined as "a simple and seemingly magical solution to a complicated problem."

Many of us are looking for a silver bullet to fix our sales, our teams, our clients, ourselves and/or our companies. When you start looking for the silver bullet, you feel like you have done everything you can to solve your challenge and yet you are unhappy because whatever you have tried just hasn't worked. You know there is something out there that will make it all better; you just haven't found it yet.

The challenge the silver bullet seekers have is that they want to keep learning new things, trying them out and having them work. This is where the challenge lies. For the silver bullet seekers is that the seeking is like taking drugs. Learning new skills works really well until learning new skills stops working. See for the silver bullet seekers there is excitement in finding new solutions and implementing them. What happens is there comes a time when it is no longer about finding new skill sets. It is about using those skill sets and start working on your mindset. It is time to start working on your Results mindset.

How do you know if you are a silver bullet seeker who's time has come to give up looking for the silver bullet and start working on your Results Mindset? You will know when the new ideas aren't flowing, and nothing seems to be working as well.

Here is the challenge. Most silver bullet seekers don't realize that this is the sign to make the shift from learning to mindset. I am not saying that you stop learning. What I am saying is that there is a time that comes that it becomes about mindset and not about skill set.

If you are a silver bullet seeker and the learning isn't working what do you do? You keep looking. You keep trying. You keep paying. I don't mean to offend; I am stating a fact. How do I know? I have watched others, and more importantly, I have done this myself.

Please heed this advice. When you start looking for the silver bullet and want to go down that path, STOP! This kind of thinking will cause more heartache than you already have. Looking for the silver bullet will cost you more money, and you will not get the results you want. How do I know? As I said before, I have traveled that path.

When I wanted to increase my business, I started reading tons of books and attending lots of workshops. I spent tens of thousands of dollars looking for the answers. I tried lots of things on my quest for the silver bullet and here is what I have learned.

There is NO Silver Bullet!

That's what I said. There is no silver bullet. There is just the bullet you have. Now what? If there is no silver bullet and the only thing I have is the bullet I already possess, what the heck is one to do?

You have to bite that bullet. What do I mean? There are no easy, fast, solutions to the problem. You can search all you want to find an easy, fast solution, but when it comes right down to it, the only solution you have is to accept the challenge: Dig down and work at it.

I have learned, when you are looking for the silver bullet, it is often an indication of something bigger you need to face. Something MAJOR needs to change and that something major is your mindset; it is not your skill set.

Your skill set is just fine. There is nothing else you can learn. That is why all of those books, workshops, etc. are not working. All of those learning opportunities are about improving your skill set; they are not about improving your mindset. Once you realize you need to switch from improving your skill set to improving your mindset, you can start reading books, attending workshops, get coaching, find an accountability partner, join a mastermind group, etc. that will improve your mindset. Only when you start working on this area, will you see improvement. This is what Results Mindset is all about.

I want you to know when you commit to developing your Results Mindset, you need to be in it for the long haul. This is not going to be solved overnight. In fact, this is something you will be managing forever. Yup, I said forever. Why? As you get more successful, the Results Mindset plays an ever-growing role in your success.

The best examples of Results Mindset are the mindsets of elite athletes and military personnel. Let me give you some examples. I don't like watching tennis. I didn't like watching golf either. When I developed my new Results Mindset, I knew I needed some role models to follow, and that is when I started watching both of these sports. Tennis and golf are both highly mentally-challenging sports. In many cases, winning or losing comes down to how you manage your mindset during the game.

Let's start with tennis. I realized some athletes could be good role models for developing my new Results Mindset when I read an article about a tennis player named Andy Murray. While Andy was a very good tennis player, he wasn't a great tennis player. The article was about how Andy hired Ivan Lendl, another famous tennis player, to be his coach. What was interesting about the article was Ivan said his coaching would be totally about the mindset. He would not step foot on the court. After reading the article, I decided to see what happened. The results? Andy was the first British tennis player to win Wimbledon in 77 years, and he won a gold medal in the Olympics. Not bad results if you ask me.

Another tennis player who shows how to handle the mental challenge is Serena Williams. Every time she hits the ball, she is managing her mindset. She talks to herself. She celebrates. She gets angry. Through the whole match, she is managing her mindset point by point. I realized from watching Serena Williams that managing our mindset is what we have to do when we are fighting to achieve the results we want.

Here is something important to note. You don't have to like someone to learn from them. Yes, that is what I said. We are very quick to judge people without considering what we can learn from them. That is your Caveman Brain working. It is judging because it is working to protect you. You not liking the person is the reaction.

You may not like Andy or Serena. I am going to challenge you on that. The reason? You can still learn from them if you let your Results Mindset take the lead and quiet your Caveman Brain. I can hear you say that I don't like tennis. Ok, I give you another sport...golf.

Pro golfers are the same as Pro tennis players. They are all working on their Results Mindset not their skill set. Watch any of them on a Sunday. Every stroke is a mindset game.

Let me give you a golf example. I have seen Jordan Spieth lose because of his mindset. What is interesting is when Jordan was interviewed about the game, he told the reporter that there were things he was going to work on for the next tournament. One week later at the next tournament, he won. What was the difference between the two weeks? Jordan told the reporters he didn't let his mindset get in his way.

Getting the results you want is about managing your mindset or what I like to call it your Results Mindset. I am not saying that you won't have to tune up your skill set from time to time. What I am saying is that when you get to this level of the game, there will be a lot more time spent on managing your mindset than learning a skill set. This is how you will get the results you want.

Here is another example of managing your mindset. I have no interest in military stuff. Those who do, know how military personnel must manage their mindset all of the time. I learned to embrace the military point of view through reading the book, *Living with a SEAL* by Jesse Itzler.

This impactful book is about an entrepreneur who hires a Navy SEAL to live in his home for a month so that he can readjust his mindset. Again, if this very successful entrepreneur is working on strengthening his mindset doesn't that tell you something? I highly recommend this book. It is excellent to see a person dealing with and strengthen his mindset.

What does Results Mindset mean to you? What this means is if you want to get more results in your life, you constantly need to work on your RESULTS Mindset and stop looking for the silver bullet.

I had a client who would call me up and ask what were my thoughts about her attending this or that workshop, conference, etc. I told her that they wouldn't make a difference. She was past that, and she had to build her RESULTS Mindset. She resisted and told me I was wrong. In fact, she decided to stop coaching with me. That happens. After a while, she called me up and asked if she could come back into the program. She told me I was right. She explained that she had spent $30,000 on all types of skill set activities and it still hadn't fixed her challenges. She realized that it was time to manage her mindset. Are you falling into the same trap as my client?

Here is one other warning sign. I often find in our coaching programs, there are people who opt out right at the point they need to switch from a skill set game to a mindset game. It is almost like there is an invisible barrier that stops them from this important breakthrough. This is an act of self-sabotaging.

I recognize how people don't' want to make this switch. If they could find the way to make the switch then their own lives would change for the better. I see it happen all the time. However, the invisible barrier is so strong that it hold these people from reaching the success that they crave.

If you are in this situation and feel like quitting, I am going to suggest that you keep moving forward. It is going to take a lot of time and effort. I am going to tell you it is worth it. The reason why I know it is worth it, is because I have taken that journey myself. I have made the switch. It took a lot of time and a lot of hard work to get to that level of success.

I also have made the decision to keep going on my success journey. That is why I use The RESULTS Formula. It is The RESULTS Formula that help me get to my success place and keeps me successful.

My clients tell me that once they make that transition, it opens up a whole new world of opportunities. Who wouldn't want that? Are you ready?

♛ GET RESULTS NOW! STEPS

1. Are you looking for the silver bullet?   Y   N

2. If so, what are you trying to accomplish?

   _____

   _____

   _____

3. What work have you done regarding you?

   _____

   _____

   _____

4. Is it time to work on your mental strength?   Y   N

5. What do you want to do to help your mindset get stronger?

   _____

   _____

   _____

CHAPTER 7

Z TO A RESULTS THINKER

"A goal is something you want to do.
A result is something you accomplish."

Jean, The Results Queen®

I am sure you are asking yourself, "what in the world is a Z to A Results Thinker?" I will explain, but before I do, I need to talk about A to Z Results Thinkers. Ah, did you just get it? If not, read on and you will.

Too many of us are not results oriented. In fact, we don't think about the result, we just go. We don't think about what we want or need to accomplish to succeed. When we think there is a problem that needs to be solved or a project we need to complete or a sale we need to close, we think we should go out and get it done. I call these people the A to Z Results Thinkers.

Most of us start out as A to Z Results Thinkers. As I said, we think there is a problem, and we just go. We start at A, and we continue until we get to an outcome. We often don't think about the outcome; we just go, thinking we will get to some outcome rather than a specific outcome.

What happens when we just go? We get stuck. We get frustrated. We stop. We get distracted. What do we do to help ourselves?

We decide we need to get organized. We make a list. Then what happens? We don't follow anything on the list, or we don't do many items on our list. Why? Maybe we didn't want to.

Maybe we just didn't think we were capable. Maybe we just gave up or worst yet, we don't get to the result we wanted at all and can't figure out how we got here. This is when we realize we are stuck.

Whatever our thoughts were during this process, we often don't end up with the result we wanted. Now we are not only stuck, but we are at the point where it is easier just to give up. Does any or all of this sound familiar?

How do I know this is what happens? I know because this is how many of my clients think and act before they start working with me. In fact, this is often the pain that makes them scream for help and is what drives them to my programs to get relief.

Here is an example of what one of my new clients said, "I made a long list and had it pinned to my wall for a couple of years. I didn't do many of the items on the list because I didn't want to, and didn't think I was capable. I was stuck, frustrated and didn't know what to do anymore." Does this sound like you as well?

This client went on to tell me, "I enrolled in your program. Sixty days later that list didn't exist anyone. By using the Z to A Results Thinking, I was able to get unstuck and complete everything on the list. Z to A Results Thinking works!"

Here is my question, if we don't focus on the specific results we want, how will we become more successful? How will we even know we are successful if we are not thinking about the results we want?

In fact, I find most of my clients just focus on the actual doing not on the actual result they want to achieve. That leads to frustration because they feel they are always doing, but not always succeeding. Does this sound familiar?

Instead of starting at A and working our way to Z, what if we started with "Z" first, so you get the outcome you want? What if you were to stop being an A to Z thinker and instead became a Z to A Results Thinker?

Z to A Results Thinking is a simple concept. What is Z to A Results Thinking exactly? Z to A Results Thinking is when you start thinking about the result before you even begin the project or solve a problem or close a sale.

I know it sounds insanely obvious. However, think about what you do. Do you just start or do you take some time to think about what you really want to accomplish? Do you look at the beginning or the end when you want to accomplish something?

If you think about reciting the alphabet, most of us would start with A and continue until we got to Z. When you become a Z to A Results Thinker, you start with Z. Z represents the outcome you want from the situation. Once you know that, you can start to work backward creating the action steps needed to achieve that outcome.

At first, Z to A Results Thinking is not always easy to implement. It will take practice. Why? Most of us have been trained to start at A and work our way to Z. Think about this. How many of us can recite the alphabet backward? Does it feel natural or unnatural? At first, we may struggle. However, with practice, we would be able to say the alphabet backward as quickly as we say it forward. Z to A Results Thinking is the same. Once you embrace it, it will be like breathing. It will just come naturally.

There is another benefit to being a Z to A Results Thinker. Remember the majority of people just start doing and not thinking about the result. If you become a Z to A Results Thinker, imagine the advantage you will have over those who do not think and implement this way.

How do you get started so you can become a Z to A Results Thinker? The first step in Z to A Results Thinking is easy and often overlooked. Think about my example of reciting the alphabet. Where do you start when you begin a project? Do you start with A? Do you start with Z? Some of us may say they start at the end, but if you do, it probably sounds something like, "We need to get more clients." Then we start working on how we can get more clients. We may say we want a certain outcome, but it is not always specific. Like the one I just stated.

Think about it. Our outcome is to get more clients. How many more clients? How much income should each client generate? What is the time period to get these new clients? I could go on, but you get the idea. Most of the time our outcomes are too general. In being a Z to A Thinker, we need to have a very specific outcome and here is the real magic, the more specific the outcome, the more likely we are to achieve it.

I want to give you another client story. See if you think this client is an A to Z Results Thinker or a Z to A Results Thinker. This client was given a warm referral. (A warm referral is a referral where the person you have been asked to call is expecting your call.) I asked my client what result did he want to achieve regarding this warm referral. He stated, "I need to reach out to her." That was it. I need to reach out to her.

Do you think this is the real result he wants? If you had a warm referral, what result would you want? Would you want a sale? Would you want a job? Would you want an introduction to another person? At this point, my client is an A to Z Results Thinker. He is not thinking at all about the outcome. He is thinking about an action step.

Take a moment and think about this. If you were in his shoes what outcome would you want? Is it the same as what he stated or something different?

As my client did, most of us would start with A and continue until we got to Z. When you are a Z to A Results Thinker, you start with Z. Remember Z represents the outcome you want from the situation. Once you know the result you want, then work backward to figure out and create your steps. You know you are at "A" when there are no more action steps to create. Keep asking yourself, "If I wanted to achieve this step, what is the step that comes before this that I would have to achieve to get to this step."

If you do this methodology, you will have a greater chance of getting to your result because you will have worked through the steps needed to get there. Let me give you some more examples, so this concept becomes even more crystal clear.

Let's say you are a salesperson. You want to make sales so you can make money. Noticed what I just said. You want to make sales (A thinking), so you can make money (Z thinking). Isn't that how most of us in sales think?

Here is another example. Let's say you are an employee in a

business, and you have been asked to complete a project. You say to yourself, "I need to get this project done for my boss." Then what do you do next? Most people think of the first step they need to do to get the project started. That's A to Z thinking. It is not Z to A Results Thinking

Here is one more example. In a recent email I received from a client, she asked, "I want to train my Client Service Director to manage all the other client service employees. Any suggestions on webinars that would be good to help him learn that skill? I don't want to spend a lot of time or money. Just want to give him a little empowerment and a few takeaways."

Is there any Z to A Results Thinking in that email? If you are writing or reading emails like this one, then you are experiencing A to Z thinking not Z to A Results Thinking. To help you understand Z to A Results thinking, I am going to breakdown this email, so you really see what I am talking about.

Let's star with the statement "I want to train my Client Service Director to manage all the other client service employees."

If the Client Services Director was trained to manage all the other client service employees, what would the result of that look like? Can you tell me what the result could be? Do you think my client stopped to think what the result looked like or did my client just go forward because there seem to be a problem with the Client Services Director?

In this scenario there could be many different results. Maybe the other employees would be able to increase client satisfaction, or maybe performance plans would be submitted on time, or maybe all the employees would come to work on time.

Since there could be many results in terms of training the Client Service Manager, if we were got this directive, what result do we want to work towards? In this case, it is hard to figure it out. If we don't know what success will look like because this person receives training as a manager, how will anyone know that this person was successful?

Let's change the statement using Z to A Results Thinking. What if I said, "My Client Service Director is currently overseeing all of the client service employees so that each one is contributing to the bottom line of the business." See the difference?

If I start using this new sentence "my Client Service Director is currently overseeing all of the client service employees so that each one is contributing to the bottom line of the business," what is the proceeding step that would need to be done? How about "everyone in the department understands what the bottom line of the business is." To be successful, the director and his employees have to know what it means to achieve it.

In this example, I would start with 1) what result you want and 2) how you know the director is successful when the director is managing the rest of the team. What does that look like to you, to the director and the staff? Once you understand this, then you can determine what skills and mindset the director has and what skills and mindset the director needs.

Using this process, you can also determine what skills and mindset the employees have and what skills and mindset the employees need. Once you know the gap, then you can offer the director specific types of learning needed to be successful.

Z to A Results Thinking makes you think first about the result each and every time. It is training your brain to think about the results first, and then the action steps second. It is a process you need to practice until it becomes as much a part of you as breathing.

Z to A Results Thinking may be a little disconcerting at first. Think about a person who is out of shape. It is difficult at first for this person to run a mile. However, with practice, they can work up to running a marathon! Z to A Results Thinking is the same process. Keep at it, and you will be amazed how you start to think differently and the results you get because of it.

Becoming a Z to A Result Thinker is not going to happen overnight. I am going to suggest that you keep practicing. The more you practice, the better you will get.

My clients tell me once they get the hang of Z to A Result Results Thinking, it is easy to do and allows them to get the results they want every time. If you are ready to give up those goals so you can get results, you need to become Z to A Result Thinker!

👑 GET RESULTS NOW! STEPS

1. **Think about a project you are currently working on.**

2. **What is the outcome you want? (Write it down below)**

_____

_____

_____

_____

3. **Is this outcome really the "Z" outcome?   Y   N**

4. **Is this outcome specific enough?   Y   N**

5. Write it again, thinking as a Z to A Results Thinker

_____

_____

_____

_____

_____

_____

_____

Is there a difference between question number 2 and question number 5? If so, take notice of what changed and make sure all of your statements going forward are results oriented.

CHAPTER 8

READY

*"When you are ready,
the teacher will appear."*

Jean, The Results Queen®

I have given you all the foundational building blocks for the Results Formula. Now that you have them, I can move on and teach you about each step in the Results Formula. If you think you need more time working on the building blocks, then stop here and spend time reviewing and understanding the building blocks of the Results Formula. If you want to get the complete system and then go back and implement it, then keep reading on.

As I stated before, the "R" in The RESULTS Formula stands for READY. Ready means you have decided you want more, and you are willing to do what it takes to get more. It means you have realized what you are doing is not working toward getting to the next level of success. You also realize it hasn't been working for some time.

This readiness can come in a couple of forms. One form is that you are ready to try something new because you have been working for quite a while and you keep doing the same things over and over again. Each time you hope for a different or even better result. Remember that is the definition of insanity: Doing the same thing over and over again hoping for a different result.

You may realize by now you have been practicing this insanity method. You now may realize it is time to stop it. It is time to get out of this endless loop and try something new that works.

This readiness could come from the fact that you have been working, and everything has gone great and then you hit a snag. You realize it is time to change because you do not want to continue down this path. You know based on hitting the wall, it is time to change what is happening.

This readiness could come from the fact that if you don't do something right now, you will be in bigger trouble than you are now. You may have been in decline for some time, and if you don't reverse direction there will be nothing left.

This readiness could also come from the fact that you just want more. You want to move to the next level of success. You can feel something inside of you that says . . . "Let's go."

All of these scenarios represent what I call the READY PEOPLE. Of course, not all people fall into this category. If I lined up ten people, six of them would be happy with what they are doing. They don't see the need to change or grow. They truly believe what they are doing right now is leading them to success. Like it or not, I would classify these people as mediocre.

That leaves four people. Two of those four are people that if they don't do something quickly they are going to fail. They are already on the slippery slope and are going downhill. They missed the point where they needed to change. Can they climb back up?

Yes, but often things are so bad that they are in crisis mode. It is hard to be ready when you are operating from crisis. You are so focused on bailing the water out of the boat, you miss the big ship going by that could save you. Like it or not, I classify these people as the slippy slope people

That leaves the other two people. These two people are "THE READY PEOPLE." The ready people are the ones who realize they must improve every day to be more successful tomorrow. These are people who know they are ready for more in life and out of their life.

These two people are ready to meet whatever challenges come their way. They are ready to change. They are ready to grow. They are ready for the next stage. They want to be more successful. They know they must be more successful, or they will end up in the mediocre category or even worse, the slippery slope group.

READY people are willing to get out of their comfort zone. They are willing to make themselves feel uncomfortable to grow. In fact, the READY people realize they have to get comfortable being uncomfortable. This is why becoming and being uncomfortable is important. The READY people know that is the only way they will grow and be more successful.

I told you I spent a whole year working on being comfortable being uncomfortable. I use that as a touch point. I know when I am uncomfortable. I know how to put myself in an uncomfortable place and be ok with it. Why? I am learning and growing when I am uncomfortable. When I am not comfortable, I am acting as a mediocre person. I don't want that. I will say this, if you can embrace being a READY person, and become a READY person, you usually stay a READY person.

That is why The RESULTS Formula starts with the word READY. If you aren't ready to make a change, then you are stuck in one of the other two categories. Unfortunately, when we are stuck in these two other categories, we have a false sense of readiness.

What do I mean by that? You may think you are ready, but things will stop you from achieving your results. When this happens, you know you are not in the READY category. When you are truly ready to grow, you will do whatever it takes.

Here's a question. Do you know people who fit into the three categories of mediocre, slippy slope, and READY? It may be easier to understand this concept if you can relate it to someone in your life.

Who do you know who is in the mediocre category? This is the person who complains about their work life. They aren't getting enough, and yet they don't want to do anything about it. Who do you know who is like that? Write that person's name down, so when you think of the mediocre person, you can say, "Oh, that is Susie."

Think of someone who is in the slippy slope category. This is the person who knows they missed the opportunity and if they don't do something tomorrow, it is all going to crash down around them. This is the person who says, "Oh I need to find a new job or a new piece of business, but I'll wait."

The problem is because they waited so long they are now in trouble. They can't find a piece of business, or they have gotten laid off from their job because they were not proactive enough. You know this person. Write their name down, so when you think of those who are on the slippery slope you think of them.

Now we have the READY People. I know you want to be in the READY category. Before we get to the "who I am," part, let's complete this exercise first.

Who do you know who is a READY person? As I have explained before, the READY person is working on improving every day so they can be more successful tomorrow. Again, I know you know someone who fits into this category. This is the person who says, "I just read this book and learned this," or they say, "I am working with a coach who helped me accomplished this." They don't let anything get in their way of improving every single day. They are not satisfied where they are, and they know they want more. Write the name of the person you know is that READY person.

Now that you have identified all three types let's continue working on you. Which group are you in? I believe you are in "THE READY PEOPLE" group. How do I know this? I know this because you are reading this book!

The RESULTS Formula will help you move to the next level and the next level and the next level. Once you complete the formula, you can (and I am going to suggest that you do) start the formula over again. The RESULTS Formula is a repeatable process. That is the reason it is successful.

The challenge will be, do you want to start the formula over again or stay where you are once you reach that new level? I know the answer for me. However, you need to decide the answer for you. There are no wrong answers. There is just an answer.

I have clients that complete the Results Formula, and then they take a break. They need to catch their breath before they start to climb to the next level of success. Other clients I have worked with keep going and going and going. The decision is up to you.

This is the thing I love about the Results Formula. It will work for anyone at any time. It works professionally or personally. It is up to you how and when you use it. Here is the thing. You have to use the whole formula. You can't use it occasionally to make it work. You have to use it every day. When you incorporate The RESULTS Formula into your life, it will become like breathing. It becomes a part of you. That is why being READY is important.

You might be ready now, and when you complete The RESULTS formula, you might move back into the "I am happy for now state." As I said before, some people need to catch their breath. Here is my warning to you, If you stay too long in the "I am happy for now state," you will slide into the mediocre group or worst. You will slide down into the slippery slope group. This group acts from the place of "Ack! If I don't do something, I am out of business." Let me give you an example of all three groups, so you can better understand.

Here is an example of the slippy slope group. I worked with a family-owned heating and cooling business. The business had been very successful in previous years. When they reached out to me, they were concerned because their business was starting to slip and they didn't want it to slip even further.

Before I go on with the story, can you see how this group was stuck in the "mediocre" level? They had years of success. What were they doing to capitalize on that success? What were they doing to grow to be even more successful? Nothing. They were just raking in the money as it came to them.

The problem with this strategy is that eventually, it will catch up to you and the money will stop flowing in. Then what? You are on the slippery slope, and no one wants to be there.

Here is what I say to all of my clients who may be moving into the mediocre category: When you are making money, and things are great, make sure you are doing everything you can to GROW.

I truly believe if you are not growing, you are dying. That is why I don't want you to wait too long after you complete The RESULTS Formula to start again. As I said before, it is easy to be comfortable. It is also easier to fall down the slippery slope when you are in that comfortable state.

Ok, back to my client story about the family-owned heating and cooling business. I told you after years of success, they reached out to me when their business starting slipping and they were losing money. Their concern was this downward trajectory would continue. Here was the problem; they weren't READY. They knew they had a problem and yet they really didn't want to change it. They said they did, but their actions showed they didn't. If you are not willing to change, what do you think is going to happen?

That is why The RESULTS Formula works. How many times have you wanted to close a sale or help an employee or a friend yet, you can't seem to get the job done? It may not be you. It may be the fact the other party is not READY. To save yourself from frustration, recognize that you have two choices. You can either help these people get ready or move on to people you can help. Some people, such as my cooling and heating company, were just not ready for help.

You may occasionally fall out of the "READY," category, and that is ok too. The RESULTS Formula will get you back on track. It is a great accountability tool to use when you fall off the path. Know that you will at some point fall off, but what is great is when you realize it, you can get back on with The RESULTS Formula.

As I said before, The RESULTS Formula is a repeatable formula. You can use it over and over again to keep yourself moving to higher and higher levels of success. I think you are starting to realize why I developed The Results Formula. I developed The RESULTS Formula to help those folks who were always saying to me, "I want to get to the next level of success." Now that you know the first step in the Results Formula, are you ready for more?

GET RESULTS NOW! STEPS

1. Write down the characteristics and actions of a READY person.

   _____

   _____

   _____

   _____

2. Write down the characteristics and actions of a MEDIOCRE person.

   _____

   _____

   _____

   _____

3. Write down the characteristics and actions of a SLIPPY SLOPE person.

   _____

   _____

   _____

   _____

4. How will you recognize a READY Person?

   _____

   _____

   _____

   _____

5. If the person is not a READY person, what can you do to get that person to become a ready person (Hint, this may be you)?

_____

_____

_____

_____

6. What are you willing to commit to, if you stop being a READY person?

_____

_____

_____

_____

CHAPTER 9

END

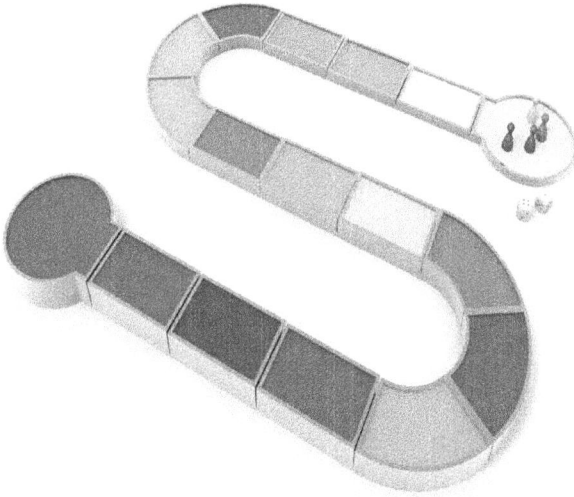

"When you start with the end in mind,
You will achieve the results you want."

Jean, The Results Queen®

The next step in The RESULTS Formula is E. E stands for END. Think about end as the end result you want to achieve. End is a definable outcome. It is specific. It tells you what you want to achieve and because it is so specific, you will know when you have successfully achieved it.

Most of my clients have to learn how to focus on the end results. Before they started working with me, most of my clients focused on general outcomes. Before I continue, I want you to stop and ask yourself if you are defining specific outcomes that you want to achieve or are you just focused on general outcomes? If you said you are defining specific outcomes, are you doing it in every part of your life? When you are able to develop the end for every part of your life, then you know you are always focused on the end results.

What do I mean by general outcomes? General outcomes sound like "I need more sales", or "I need to get the project completed by a certain deadline". I don't consider these statements to be specific. I don't even think of these statements as results oriented. Here is the reason why you need to be as specific as you can be. The more specific you are in telling your brain what you want, the more likely you are to achieve it. While I can't tell you how it works, I can tell you that if your brain knows what you want to achieve, it will help you achieve it.

I want more sales is not a specific end result statement. It is just a statement. Many of my clients speak this way before they start working with me. They often say these general statements with the hopes of getting a result. Unfortunately these general statements only left them feeling stuck and frustrated.

How do you know you have gotten to the end result when you say something like, "I need more sales?" You need to define what the result would look like if you were to get more sales. If you were coaching with me, I would ask you:

- How much
- How many
- With whom
- In what industry
- With what product and/or service

…You get the picture.

How do you end this frustration? You have to start training yourself to think about the end before you start. The problem many of my clients were having was due to the fact they haven't trained themselves to think about the end first. They just started. They didn't take the time to define what the end looked like for them.

Does this sound familiar to you? Are you in the same boat? Are you defining the end or just starting at the beginning?

I define the end as the result that I want to achieve. As you do all of your activities, I am going to ask you to keep the end in your mind — always. To me, it is always about the result. It is always about the result. It is always about the endgame.

If you can train yourself to always start with the end in mind, you will accomplish a lot more. Why? Those who know what the end result looks like get the end result they want because they can see what the end result looks like. In some cases they can feel or smell or taste what the end result looks like. In any event, those who have trained themselves to always start with the endgame, get the end game.

How do they do this? They use a technique called visualization. Visualization is an important part of achieving the results you desire. Unfortunately, most people don't visualize because they don't know the outcome they want or they have never used visualization techniques to help get them to that result. Worst, some people think it takes too much time to stop and visualize so they just don't do it.

For those of you who don't know visualization techniques, let me explain. Visualization is when you take the time to see in your mind's eye or put pictures down on a piece of paper or type out in words what the end result looks like.

Many people use visualization techniques to create something called vision boards. I have one that I look at every morning and every evening. The vision board can have words or pictures or both. I create a new one every year. I cut pictures and words out from magazines, I paste them onto the board. I hang it up in a place so I can see it every day. At the end of the year, before I create the next board, I review what results I have achieved based on what I put on my vision board. I am always amazed at the results.

One thing I have learned about visualization is that it works really well with your brain. Your brain loves pictures and the better picture you can create in your brain, the more likely you are to achieve that picture. That's why it is important to take the time and develop what your end looks like for each project.

Now I am going to ask you to take a moment. Think about what you do when you need to achieve something. Have you ever thought about what it takes to get the results you want? Have you ever thought about what your end result looks like? Do you understand what it is going to take to get there? Will you even know what it looks like when you get there?

In business, how many of us are ALWAYS looking toward the end? How many of us even think about the end result? How many of us even know the result we want to achieve?

Let me put it this way. Image what it would be like to always get to the outcome that you want? What would your life be like? How would you be better?

Too many of us are not end result oriented. As I said before, we don't think about the end at all. We just go. We don't think about what we want or need to accomplish to succeed. We don't take the time to think about the result and what it means and what it will take to get there. When you just go, where do you end up?

Not at the place you really wanted to be.

For many of us, when we think there is a problem we need to solve or a project we need to complete or a sale we need to close, we think we should go out and get it done. What happens when we just go? Sometimes we get lucky, and we get to the result. However, more often than not, we get stuck. We get frustrated. We get distracted. We never achieve what we truly wanted.

What do we do to help ourselves? We decide that we need to get organized. We make a list. We recommit to move forward because we have to. We have bills to pay. We have family that needs us. We know there is more for us than just this.

Then what happens? We don't do many items on our list or worse we don't follow anything on the list or even worse than that, we stop. Once we stop, we don't normally start again. Why? Maybe we don't want to. Maybe we just don't think we are capable. Maybe we just give up or worst yet, we don't get to the outcome we wanted at all and can't figure out how we got here.

Whatever our thoughts were during this process, we often don't end up with the result we wanted. We don't get to our end result. We don't achieve our outcome. Now we are not only stuck, but we are at the point where it is easier just to give up. Does any or all of this sound familiar?

If we don't focus on the specific results we want, how will we become more successful? How will we even know we are successful if we are not thinking about the results we want?

As I said before, I find many people just focus on the actual doing not on the actual results they want to achieve. They don't define their end. They don't define the result. They don't think about what it will take to get there, and they certainly don't think about how to overcome the obstacles I know they are going to encounter because there are always obstacles along the way.

The lack of planning leads to frustration because they feel they are always doing, but not always succeeding. Does this sound familiar as well?

As you use The Results Formula, you will realize when you define your end result, you will achieve the outcomes you want. It is not an overpromise. I have been teaching The RESULTS Formula to my clients with amazing…well results. When you use The RESULTS Formula all the time, you will get better results for yourself and those around you.

I was working with a client recently, and we were discussing how she should improve her end results. As a high-powered attorney, she was highly successful. However, she wasn't always getting the results she wanted in her sales. Why? She winged it. Her style worked well for a very long time until it stopped working. Have things stopped working for you? Could it be that you have been winging it and that technique is not working as well as it once did? If you are winging it, how are you achieving results, consistently?

Marshall Goldsmith, a very famous executive coach, who I have worked with, once said, "What got you to this place won't get you to the next place." I agree with him. When you want more than what you have now, you need to change what you are doing, learn new skills and strengthen your mindset."

For this high-powered lawyer, I asked her to figure out what the end results were before every meeting. I did this because when we first started working together, she told me what her sales activities were and commented, "I got this." However, as I started to ask questions around her end results, it became clear to both of us that she didn't "have it."

The reason she didn't have it was because she wasn't thinking about the end results all the time. She didn't take the time to develop these results. She just thought she had it and she could just wing it. She was using something I call the ad-lib technique.

How did she switch from the ad-lib technique to The Results Formula? She started to realize when you take the time to strategize about the end, you get better results because you know what you are striving for rather than making it up in the moment.

As my example shows, you must start thinking about the end and the results before you even begin the project or solve a problem or close a sale. My example also shows, it is not always easy to put into practice. Why? It takes time. It also takes effort. Most of us are not good at taking time because we don't think we have enough time. We just want to get it done. That is why sometimes we don't take the time to stop and think about what the result we want to achieve. Many of us think getting something done is more important than spending time thinking about results.

I am going to tell you the more time you spend on developing yourself in Z to A Results thinking, the easier and faster it will be to achieve the result you want. If you spend the time thinking, you will have figured out everything that could happen and have the correct responses already thought out before you start. When you do this every time, you will soon realize that when you put that into play, the actual implementation becomes much easier and much more consistent.

It doesn't matter if you think of results as the "end" or the "endgame," or "the result" or even "the outcome". I like the word "result" because it tells my Caveman Brain what we are working to achieve. For the results- focused people, it is consistently about the results and making sure they achieve them. The reason they are successful is because they know what the result is and they are ready to go get them. If you want to achieve "the end" use the Z to A Result Thinking method I taught you previously and you will always have the "end" in mind.

♕ GET RESULTS NOW! STEPS

1. Write down a current activity you are working on.

_____

_____

_____

_____

_____

2. What is your endgame for this activity?

_____

_____

_____

_____

3. If you could only get the minimum result what would that be?

_____

_____

_____

_____

_____

4. What obstacles could get in the way of achieving your ultimate endgame or your minimum result?

_____

_____

_____

_____

_____

5. What would you need to do or say to overcome those obstacles?

_____

_____

_____

_____

CHAPTER 10

STEPS

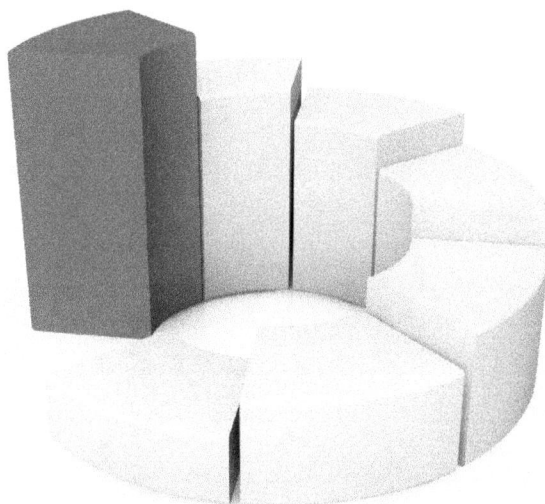

*"Taking that first step brings you
closer to your result."*

Jean, The Results Queen®

The "S" in The RESULTS formula stands for "Steps." A helpful hint is thinking about the steps as action steps. The more specific you make these actions steps, the more likely you will achieve the results.

Let's talk about "steps" or what I will refer to as action steps. How many times do you write all of your action steps down? Let me ask this question in a different way. Are you the person who writes down every single action or are you someone who just wings it or are you doing a bit of both?

At this point, I hope you are starting to realize that if you are winging it in any way shape of form, that methodology won't yield the result you want because you haven't thought about everything it takes to get to the result you want.

This is where actions steps come in. Once you define the result or the end, you must immediate define the action steps to get you there. This is where you can implement your Z to A Results Thinking method.

When you are developing your action steps, you need to start working backward developing the specific steps needed to achieve the result you desire. Start with Z, and keep working backward developing the action steps needed until you get to A. Once you have all of the steps defined, then you can start playing them forward by starting with the step that you defined as A and continuing until you get to Z.

This can be confusing to some of you. Here is the step by step process to help you develop action steps. This is a repeatable process.

Step 1

The first step in this process is to write down your end result. Now think about what would it take to get that result. Write that down. That is one of your action steps. Now reflect on this action step and think about what it would take for you to accomplish that action step. Write that down. This becomes another action step. Notice that I am working backward. You keep applying this process until you have all the steps needed to accomplish the result you want. Obviously, your action steps will be out of order because you worked backward. There is a very simple solution to this. Now that you have all of your action steps written down, you just work them forward. Because you worked backward to get there, you know what it takes to get to the results, so going forward is now easier.

Step 2

The second step in this process is to put dates next to these action steps to ensure they get done. Now you can figure out the dates either by working backward or forward. If you have a firm end date, then you should start from that date and work backward as you figure out what dates should go with what activities. You may not always know the end date. If that is the case, work forward. Either way, you must put dates to your action steps.

This brings me to a question you may be asking yourself. Should my dates be in hours, days, weeks, months, quarters or years? The answer is . . . it depends. You decide what you can sustain. You decide what will motivate you to achieve those action steps. In other words, there is no right or wrong way to develop your action steps dates; it is up to you. You decide what makes sense for you.

Step 3

The third step in the process is to take your action steps dates and develop a timeline. To create a timeline, put the dates in the proper order from start to finish.

That is the thinking part of the system. Holding yourself accountable is the action part of the process. We have talked a lot about the thinking part in this book, let's to talk about the action part. After all this is the "action steps" part of the book.

What I want you to realize is that action steps is a two part process. There is the thinking part and there is the implementation part. Many people just do the implementation and not the thinking.

There are others that start the implementation part and don't always finish it. That is why accountability is important when you are implementing action steps.

Holding yourself accountable seems to be one of the hardest things for many of us to do. I know I have a hard time with that as well. Remember the horse book I spoke about? The book that said the thing that horses and human have in common? The book that said horses and humans are lazy? I think that is at the heart of accountability being hard.

Think about it. Would you rather sit around and watch TV or go out and run a marathon? For a few of us, we are in the latter category. For many of us, we are in the former. Often, the difference between the two makes or breaks success.

I spoke about Serena Williams before. She is the world-class tennis player. She once said even she had to make the conscious choice of going out with her friends or getting on the court to practice. I am sure she would have rather chosen to be with her friends, but knowing her choice to practice contributed to her being the best in the world, she chose practice over socializing.

We all have the same choice as to how we hold ourselves accountable. I will tell you I am not very good at it. Yes, really. Since I know this about myself, I have put systems in place to make sure I am being held accountable.

If you can hold yourself accountable, then I applaud you. If, like me, you find it difficult, then let me give you some tips to help you in that area.

Once you realize you could use some support in the accountability arena, you need to decide what type and how much. Many people think their boss will hold them accountable and that could be true. However, if you are not being held accountable, then you may need someone outside of your team to take on that role.

I know that many want to start with the free option and I am ok with that as a first step. Please remember you get what you pay for. If you don't have a lot of money to spend, then find someone who can be your accountability partner or develop a mastermind group. I have done both without paying, and both have worked out great for me. I was successful in this because I was careful about who I chose to help me. I know I have spoken about this before, but let me give you more detail on how to successfully find and implement both.

An accountability partner is someone you ask to help you be more accountable. In most cases, this person is someone you do not pay. When picking an accountability partner, write down what you want your accountability partner to do for you. Then write down what you are willing to do to for your accountability partner.

Next, you need to find a person who fits your requirements. Once I figured out my requirements, it took me two years to find the right accountability partner. It could take you less time or more. What I will tell you is once you commit, then stay committed until you find that person.

Once you have found an accountability partner, then meet to discuss what you want to accomplish, what they want to accomplish and how you will work together. When I work with my accountability partner, we speak every single day. I know that others who have accountability partners speak once a week or once a month. Again, it depends on what you are willing to commit to. I have found having an accountability partner has made a big difference in what I accomplish, and I am sure it will help you as well.

Let's talk about finding a mastermind group. This could be a group you paid to be a part of or not. I have done both. I have experienced success in both types of groups. It is up to you and how you want to proceed.

Just like with an accountability partner, you need to determine your requirements and find a group that will meet them. A lot of times the success of a mastermind group will come down to the chemistry of the people in that group. Make sure there are people who are willing to hold you accountable to achieve your results before you jump in and start.

Now that I have spoken about accountability partners and mastermind groups, let me give two other ways to hold yourself accountable. 1) Customer Relationship Management (CRM) systems. I have used a variety of them, and the ones I like best are the ones that send you a daily reminder of what to do. 2) Your calendar. I use my daily calendar to hold me accountable. My calendar reminds me to conduct specific activities. I color code my calendar so with just a glance I know what I am doing. You can use this method to accomplish the activities you need to achieve the results you want.

Being accountable is as important as developing your action steps. As I said before, I know I need to have accountability systems to be held accountable. I also know for myself, I need a bunch of systems to be successful. You may need one system or several. There is no right or wrong way. There is just the right way for you. I would suggest that you experiment to gain an understanding of what works.

No matter how you hold yourself accountable, you need to review your action steps either daily or weekly to keep them top of mind. When you don't keep your action steps top of mind, they will end up not getting done. What's the point of putting in all of this work if you are not going to use it to accomplish your result?

To be successful in the "steps" part of The RESULTS Formula, remember the two parts. Develop the action steps and then implement the actions steps. If you have trouble developing them then Use the Z to A Results Thinking Method. If you have trouble implementing the action steps. Find some one to hold you accountable.

♛ GET RESULTS NOW! STEPS

1. **Here is your chance to start working on your action steps. Write them all down here:**

_____

_____

_____

_____

_____

_____

_____

_____

2. How are you going to hold yourself accountable?

_____

_____

_____

_____

_____

_____

_____

_____

_____

_____

CHAPTER 11

YOU

"Managing YOU may be the toughest and most rewarding part of achieving the next level of success."

Jean, The Results Queen®

The "U" in The RESULTS Formula stands for "You." As I explained previously, I took some poetic license, given that we use the letter "U" to indicate the word "you".

Obviously to achieve greater results you need to be involved. During your RESULTS journey, you must also work on yourself and your abilities. You need to work on the specific skills you need to achieve the results you desire. This includes both skill set and mindset. Remember you will always be working on mindset. Working on your skill set will depend upon where you are in your abilities.

As I said before, the problem is once we graduate from school, many of us stop investing in ourselves. We stop learning. We don't pay the money to buy a book or go to a workshop or take a class or get a degree. In fact, for some of us, we get angry we have to learn new stuff. Why? It takes time to learn new things and for many of us, time is a big issue. Why is time an issue? Well, we have so many other things to achieve. We don't have time to focus on this new stuff.

I have seen many people become downright resentful that they have to take time from their schedule to learn something new. I understand because I have been that person. When I was working in my corporate job, senior management had put together a training program that was to help those at my level be more successful. It wasn't mandatory. Since I wasn't required to go, I decided to opt out because I had so much more work to accomplish and I just couldn't figure out where to fit this training program into my schedule.

Guess what happened? I missed out. I missed out on learning new information that could have helped my career. I missed out on showing senior management I wanted to be more successful at the company. I missed out on strengthening relationships. I missed out on a whole lot. I never did that again because missing out sucks.

The lesson I learned is when you least want to do something, it is probably an indication you need to do it! The bottom line is…if you are seeking greater outcomes, then you must invest in yourself. Don't miss the opportunity when it presents itself.

Investing in yourself isn't difficult unless you make it difficult. "I don't have the time." I don't have the money." "I don't think can do it". These are all statements that either you say out loud or internally that makes it difficult. Remember Caveman Brain? When you hear these statements, then implement your RESULTS mindset and The RESULTS Formula to invest in yourself and get yourself on the or back on the RESULTS journey.

What do I mean by that? As I said before, many of us don't invest in ourselves, and there are many reasons for this including time, money, not believing in ourselves or a lack of confidence. There are lots of other factors too, but you get the picture.

There are two major factors that go into managing you. The first is building your skill set, and the second is building your mindset. While I have discussed both of these in previous chapters, it bears saying again because both will make an impact on your results.

Remember when I told you when you get to a certain level, it becomes less about your skill set and more about your mindset. In fact, I said when you get to a certain level it is ALL about your mindset, and it will continue to be all about your mindset until you decide to stop your RESULTS journey.

What do you need to do to manage you? I have given you the ideas of an accountability partner and being a part of a mastermind group. There are several other things you can do to add to your success abilities.

You can build and strengthen your community of support. A community of support is hanging out with like-minded people who share your values and attitudes toward success. Where can you find a community of support? Trade associations, chambers of commerce, even coaches have communities you can become part of. You just need to find the one that suits you and join it. If it doesn't work for you, keep looking and keep trying new communities until you find a good fit.

Build a team around you. Think about the most successful people. They have a team around them. When I think of a team of support, I think of Daria Torres. Daria Torres was an Olympic swimmer who decided at the age of 41 to swim in the Olympics. For her to do that successfully, she built a team around her that supported her efforts. She ended up with a silver medal.

Do you have a team around you? I think a team is different than a community. A team is a select group of people who work together to support you. This could be a group of employees, an advisory board or those you hire to assist you…like a coach.

Many of us think we don't need a coach. We think that if we have a coach, something is wrong with us. In fact, I had a client who was a financial advisor. I was working with her and some of her colleagues in her organization. She wrote an email to her senior management that the company would need to figure out how to support their sales activities with out me.

On our next call I asked her if she told her clients that there would be a time when they would not need a financial advisor in their lives and they would be able to handle all of their financial activities on their own. My client said that was ridiculous. Why would she tell her clients that. They needed her to be more successful. I asked her what was the difference between having a financial advisor and having a coach. She paused and said to me, "If I want to continue to be successful, I am going to always need a coach." I told her, "Yes.". You see my point.

Someone "coaching" has been associated with remedial. I am going to suggest that if you think this way, that you may want to start thinking that "coaching" keeps you on the cutting edge, innovative and successful.

From the day I started my business to today, I have always had a coach. I'm from the world where having a coach is a necessity. I once was a musician and played the string bass. All great musicians have a coach or mentor they work with to get better. Pavarotti had a coach. Leonard Bernstein had a coach and was also a coach. As a musician, you need someone else listening to your music to provide insights on where to get better, and being the best in your field is no different. I believe you need an outside person looking in to give you the insights on where you are doing well and where you need to improve. Let me give you a story of how a coach can help you and what happens when you let that coach go.

Right after I had children, I decided to hire a personal trainer. Remember how I enjoyed running right? Well, I really hate exercising too. I worked with my personal trainer to eat healthily and to get and keep my butt in great shape. However, as I got more successful, I didn't have the time to be all in, and so I let my personal trainer go.

It was my intention to exercise every day, and I thought I could exercise on my own. I joined a gym. I bought P90X. I had my girlfriend call me up to keep me accountable. Guess what? I gained 15 pounds. It was still my intention to exercise every day, but other things got in the way. Can you relate?

My experience is that when I had a personal trainer I was more successful in living a healthy lifestyle. When I didn't have a personal trainer in my life, I just wasn't able to achieve the same results. It was based on this experience that I realized how important it is to have a coach in your life.

I view having a business coach the same way. You need someone who inspires you. You need someone who pushes you, encourages you and gets into the deep water with you to help you navigate your way out. You need a sounding board. You need someone who has the experience you want to have. You need someone who is willing to teach you and tell you about the pitfalls, so you don't have to experience them. I once saw an ad that said, "It takes someone strong to make someone stronger." I believe that is true.

I truly believe everyone can benefit from a coach. I have a willingness to seek out the help others can provide me. Do you have the wiliness to do that too?

My very first team member was a business coach. You may pick a different team member like a financial professor or an assistant. For me, I needed another person to manage me! You may be in the same place.

Why do you need a team, a community, a coach and everything else? Managing you can be hard work. It can be especially hard on your own as you become more successful. Those who know they need other around tem become more successful then those who try to do it alone.

Remember I spoke about Serena Williams? She filmed a documentary about coming back to tennis after she had a baby. There was a segment when her coach had a real heart to heart talk. Serena had a choice. She could stay with her coach and make the comeback to number one or she could just play good tennis and get a different coach. What do you think her decision was? Having someone else to manage you can help you to scc things that you can't see.

Here is a mindset activity to help you in managing you. Think about the idea of being a champion every day. Imagine if you were the best at your game every day. How would you act? What would you do? I challenge you to wake up each day and be a champion for your life!

The last idea I want to give you might be the most important. It involves grit. The dictionary defines grit as a noun and a verb. When you use grit as a noun, it is defined as: courage and resolve; strength of character. When you use grit as a verb, it is defined as: clench the teeth, especially to keep one's resolve when faced with an unpleasant or painful duty. In other words, you can define grit as your mental toughness. Mental toughness is the most important factor in managing you. There is more and more research on grit. I suggest that you read more about it and implement grit into your life.

If I haven't given you enough to help you be a better you, let me provide a checklist that you can use to rate yourself. According to Dennis Charney of the Icahn School of Medicine at Mount Sinai in New York City, there are ten factors that keep us going despite all odds. Scoring high in these factors can determine your success. I am going to suggest that you use these ten factors as a checklist to see how you are doing in developing you. When you can score and maintain a ten on all of these factors consistently, I am going to bet you are in the game of keeping you strong. Here are the ten factors. They include:

- Facing fear

- Having a moral compass

- Drawing on faith

- Using social support

- Having good role models

- Being physically fit

- Making sure your brain is challenged

- Displaying "cognitive and emotional flexibility"

- Having "meaning, purpose and growth" in life

- Showing "realistic" optimism

As I said, I would suggest you rate yourself on these factors from one to ten where one is the lowest and ten is the highest. Once you have done that, pick the three you want to strengthen and work on them. Notice I didn't say improve. I don't think it is important to make weaknesses stronger. I think it is important to make your strengths stronger. Pick the ones you want to make stronger and start working. Once you get them to where you want them, pick the next three. Keep working until you have completed the entire list.

Once you have completed the list, re-rate yourself. If you don't score tens in all categories, start over again. If you do score tens in all areas, then figure out how you are going to maintain all those tens and keep at it. I would suggest that you keep rating yourself every 90 days to ensure you are staying at the top of your game. If you score something lower than ten, you know what to do. Start working on that area. I think this list can be used forever. That's my opinion; I will let you decide how you want to implement this idea.

YOU are the most important part of The RESULTS Formula. You have to do the heavy lifting for yourself. If you aren't willing to commit to yourself then no matter what you do, you won't be able to achieve all of the results you are meant to achieve.

I believe we are all here on this earth to accomplish something and not to waste our lives. Being the best is not only a gift to yourself, but it is also a gift to the world. Please do what it takes to improve yourself because as YOU improve your results will improve as well.

👑 GET RESULTS NOW! STEPS

1. **Rate your grit and then decide what you need to work on. Keep working your plan so your grit is always a ten.**

   - Facing fear
   - Having a moral compass
   - Drawing on faith
   - Using social support
   - Having good role models
   - Being physically fit
   - Making sure your brain is challenged
   - Displaying "cognitive and emotional flexibility"
   - Having "meaning, purpose and growth" in life
   - Showing "Realistic" optimism

2. **How are you going to build your community?**

   _____

   _____

   _____

   _____

   _____

3. What do you need to do to improve your skill set and your mindset?

_____

_____

_____

_____

_____

4. Are you getting the coaching you need and if not, are you ready to get the right coach for you?   Y or N?

5. If you said no, what is holding you back?

_____

_____

_____

_____

_____

6. If you said yes, what do you need to get from your coach to move you forward to the RESULT you want?

_____

_____

_____

_____

_____

CHAPTER 12

LEVELS OF LEARNING

"Levels of Learning never stops
when you commit to getting results!"

Jean, The Results Queen®

The "L" in The RESULTS Formula stands for "Levels of Learning." Because you are ready, you thought about the end result you want to achieve; you took the time to create and implement specific action steps and you are focused on improving yourself. Now you are going to start going through different levels of learning.

I define levels of learning as the different phases you go through as you acquire better skills and a stronger mindset. You may feel uncomfortable at this time. You may feel frightened or frustrated because you are not sure this process is working. You may experience highs, and you may experience lows. This process is all part of the levels of learning. You are trying different ideas, and improving different skills. You will fail, and you will be successful.

Levels of learning can be informal or formal. You can go back to school to get a higher degree, or you can read a book. You can attend a workshop or listen to an expert in your field. Levels of learning can happen anywhere and anytime as long as you are ready to receive the wisdom that is coming your way.

In this stage, the most important thing is that you are learning! I urge you to embrace the concept that you should never stop learning. Not only do I urge you never to stop learning, but I strongly suggest you make the commitment to become and stay a lifelong learner. Why?

Successful people never stop learning. Successful people are always learning. They are always growing. To achieve the results you want, you have to continue to grow. I truly believe the way we grow is to commit to learning.

With that said, I also want you to remember the silver bullet syndrome I spoke about earlier. When you commit to levels of learning, you need to understand you are committing to the right learning, not just any learning. What's the difference?

When you are committed to levels of learning, you know there isn't a silver bullet out there to fix what needs fixing. You realize you have to work to get the results you want. When you are in levels of learning, you realize it is about you and what you need to learn to become more successful. It is going to take work. That is why I strongly suggested you commit to lifelong learning because once you start working on the thing you need to learn, you are going to find out you will get to a new level where you need to learn something new to continue your growth.

Where do you start? Knowing where to start depends on where you are. Go back and look at your action steps. Those action steps will tell you where to start. Look at what you wrote about yourself. That's another place to start. Remember I wrote earlier about skill set and mindset. Where you start depends on if you are starting with your skill set, your mindset or both.

Yes, you can start on both. With my clients, I often find starting with both is the best way to start. Why? Once you start working on your skill set, you are going to find that it is also your mindset holding you back from moving forward. How do I know that? Mindset is something that always needs to be strengthened. As I said before, eventually, it all becomes about your mindset.

When you work on your mindset, you will find your mind will continue to expand, and you will want to learn something new. That is why I have my clients work on both. There is no right or wrong way. The only thing you need to do is get started and always be a lifelong learner.

As part of this stage, use your action steps to get you through your levels of learning. Your action steps are very important in The RESULTS Formula because they identify the areas where you need to grow. If you don't think your action steps are strong enough, then go back and strengthen them. If you feel your action steps are strong, this is the place where you are going to put them in action. Your Levels of Learning are what will bring you greater success. Let me give you an example.

One thing that often comes up when my clients work with me is the feeling of being overwhelmed. Most of us think that being overwhelmed is a bad thing. I want to change your thinking about that.

Here are my thoughts about being overwhelmed. I used to think being overwhelmed was a bad thing too. When I felt overwhelmed, it was because I just didn't know what to do. There was so much, and often, it involved things I had never done before. One day I was complaining to my coach I was feeling overwhelmed, and she squealed with delight. I asked her why she was so excited. She told me she was excited that I was overwhelmed. Here's what I thought, "How can anyone be excited about being overwhelmed?"

She informed me when you feel overwhelmed it is because you have entered a new level of success. Since everything I was doing was new, how would I know exactly how to do those new things? Being overwhelmed was something to embraced not to complain about.

I thought about this new way of thinking. I had been using the phrase, "being overwhelmed" and actually feeling that way for an incredibly long time. How was I going to describe how I felt when there was so much to do?

After thinking about this for a long time, I decided to start tracking when I felt or said I was overwhelmed and what was attached to that. It turned out that in all cases when I felt overwhelmed it was because I was doing something new. That was an eye opener for me.

I would challenge you to do the same. When you say you are

overwhelmed, or you are feeling overwhelmed, stop. Take stock of what you are doing. Is it something new or something you have always done and yet there is just more of it? I think you will find when you are overwhelmed it is because of the newness of your activities.

Once I realized being overwhelmed was tied to my doing new activities, I decided to embrace being overwhelmed and even celebrate it because being overwhelmed showed me something. It showed me I was growing. I decided if I had too many of the same tasks to accomplish in a period of time I would call that being overloaded. If I was overloaded I needed to look at my list of activities, and either start delegating to others or exam them to see if they were worth doing.

Once I started using the words "overwhelmed" and "overloaded" in the way I described above, things started to change. I stopped being "overwhelmed." I also stopped being overloaded. How did that happen?

Every time I felt or said I was overwhelmed, I celebrated. I visibly celebrated. I danced. I shouted in joy. I sang. I bought myself a present. Sometimes it was a big present, and sometimes it was a little present. Whatever the size of the present or physical activity I did, I anchored my being overwhelmed to being a great thing.

What do I mean by anchoring it? To me, anchoring is when

you marry your celebration to something you do or to an object. You will read more about anchoring in the Success Celebration chapter. Just know that anchoring activities tells your brain this is important.

I now teach my clients about being overwhelmed and overloaded, but I wait until they bring it up. When they do bring it up, I celebrate and what I get back is so interesting. Most are in disbelief just like I was when my coach celebrated my being overwhelmed.

When my clients realize what I did about being overwhelmed and being overloaded, they are amazed. When they start using the words in the way I have described, they fully understand the amazement. They welcome being overwhelmed because they know they are growing and are becoming even more successful. Try it. I am sure you will be amazed too.

What I just described to you about being overwhelmed and being overloaded was a Level of Learning for me. I wanted you to see what a Level of Learning can be. Noticed that in that specific Level of Learning it was a mindset lesson. There wasn't any skill set learning involved.

I had to learn to think differently. I had to learn to look at things differently. I had to recognize things differently. I had to talk about things differently. All of these are mindset activities. As I have said before and I will continue to say, getting the results you want comes down to growing and managing your mindset.

I can assure you that your results will always be better if you are on a growth path rather than a stagnant path. The choice is yours. With that said, once you experience Levels of Learning, you realize the importance of continuing them because they are the keys to your success.

Levels of Learning can happen quickly, or they can take a long time. You can be working on one thing or multiple things. It is your choice as to what you work on when you are in Levels of Learning. Also note, you may be working on a Level of Learning without even being aware of it until it hits you over the head. No matter how you are going through the Levels of Learning one thing is for certain. When you have completed your Level of Learning, you will be transformed.

♛ GET RESULTS NOW! STEPS

1. **Do you believe your action steps are strong enough to take you through your Levels of Learning?**

   _____

   _____

   _____

   _____

2. **If not, then go back and rework them.**

3. How are you going to use your action steps to go through your Levels of Learning?

_____

_____

_____

_____

4. How will you recognize when you are overwhelmed vs. overloaded?

_____

_____

_____

_____

CHAPTER 13

TRANSFORMATION

"Transformation just sneaks up on you until you can't remember who you used to be."

Jean, The Results Queen®

The "T" in The RESULTS Formula stands for "Transformation." When we go through Levels of Learning, we can't help but be transformed. We will experience a new way of thinking and a new way of being.

Transformation means change. I know there are many people who are afraid of change. If you are one of these people, I am going to tell you something . . . change is a part of life. Don't believe me? Ask yourself what has changed in life since you were a kid? Cell phones, televisions, computers, space travel, even electricity was once a new thing. I could go on, but I think you get the picture.

We experience change every day. The changes I mentioned above have transformed and are transforming our lives. We are happy to have them! Why be afraid of change when you know change can make your life better?

Knowing that change can make our lives better, why do we avoid change? If we experience change every day, then why do so many of us fear change? If you are afraid of change, I believe someone or some event made you fear change. There is something in your past that makes you hate change. You can explore that thought or take it on faith. When I speak to my clients about what is holding back their transformation, it is always something that happened in their past either from a person or an event.

How do we handle the negative experience of change? We make up stories about how much we hate change. We tell ourselves how much we hate change until it becomes a part of our daily mantra. Now every time the word change comes up, we mutter to ourselves, "I hate change."

We keep telling ourselves this same story over and over again until there is nothing else to do but believe the story we have told ourselves a thousand times. The story becomes ingrained in us. It becomes part of who we are. We hold on to it like our security blanket. Here is the interesting part, we hold on to it even if we don't like it. We hold on maybe because it is familiar to us or we hold on because it is all we know. Maybe it's a little of both.

Remember when I told you your brain only believes what it hears and what it sees? Remember when I spoke about OPB? When you tell yourself the same story over and over again, the brain has no choice but to believe what you are telling it. That story becomes part of you. However, there is a way you can change that story and embrace change . . . if you want to.

You that you can change your way of thinking and you do that by changing the story you are telling yourself. When you start telling your brain a new story, your brain will start to believe it.

This is why the Levels of Learning are so important. When you open your mind to new possibilities, you are starting to change the way you think. This means you are also replacing all of those old thoughts, sayings, and feelings holding you back with new thoughts, sayings, and feelings that will propel you forward. When this happens, you are transforming.

That is why I view change as a great thing because when I am changing, I am transforming. In fact, the only way to transform is through change, so if you are saying you hate change, I suggest you start telling yourself a new story.

Transformation is an extremely important part of The RESULTS Formula. Transformation means you have moved into a new level of success. When you constantly and consistently transform, you will be even more successful. If you want to transform, you have to embrace change. That is why transformation has to be part of The RESULTS Formula. If you are not transforming then, you are not growing.

How do you know you are transforming? There are several ways to track transformation. One way is to write down where you are now and then measure that activity at another point in time. For example, I go to the same conference every year at the same time. When I go to that conference, I think about where I was the year before and then measure it against where I am now. Invariably, I have changed. I am in a different place. I call this milestone measuring. You measure yourself against the different milestones of your life.

While milestone measuring is a less formal way of measuring transformation, there is a more formal method. I call it my 90-Day Leap Forward Results Action Plan. This plan asks you to measure where you are now and then decide where you want to be in 90 days. Based on those two data points, you then develop specific action steps to ensure you will get the results you want to achieve in that 90-day period. If you would like a copy of the plan along with the instructions, please email info@getmoreresults.com, and I'll send you a copy.

There is another way to know you are transforming. It is perhaps the easiest way. Remember my story about learning the difference between being overwhelmed and overloaded? Let's go over it again. I used to say I was overwhelmed all the time until I asked my coach what to do about it. She got excited, which baffled me. Why would anyone get excited about being overwhelmed?

What she told me was that being overwhelmed was a great thing and I should embrace it. She explained that being overwhelmed meant I had transformed to the next level of success.

The reason I was feeling overwhelmed was simple. I was in a new stage, and I wasn't very good at navigating it. I was still learning the right skill set and mindset to handle this new stage successfully and comfortably.

From that point on if I said to myself, out loud or to anyone else that I was overwhelmed, I changed my thinking. I saw this feeling of being overwhelmed as a sign of transformation I needed to embrace. I also realized this was a milestone measurement. I could start tracking how many times I was feeling overwhelmed and equate that to the fact that I was learning and growing.

I do practice what I preach. See how I started to change the story I was telling myself about being overwhelmed versus being overloaded? I was feeling an emotion, which I then labeled as being overwhelmed because our Caveman Brains like to compartmentalize everything. Our brain does that as part of our survival system. Remember Caveman Brain is there to protect us. It operates on the subconscious level. So it is always working to make sure we are safe. It is one of the reasons we label stuff so our brains can figure out if it is safe or not.

After I had labeled this emotion of being overwhelmed, every time I felt it, I reinforced that this was a positive thing. Remember from the Caveman Brain chapter that changing the negative to the positive can help you achieve greater success?

We have patterns we are not even aware of because we are operating from the subconscious. Once we are aware of these patterns, we can then change them, fix them, eliminate them and/or create new patterns that will support where we want to go.

Coaches, mastermind groups and/or accountability partners can help us recognize these patterns when we can't see them. They can help us replace old patterns with new ones that serve us more in the place we currently find ourselves. That is why I think it is important to have a coach, an accountability partner, and/or a mastermind group.

Going through transformation is not always easy. Sometimes it feels like a grind. If you feel this way, keep going. It will get better. Sometimes transformation happens quickly, and it dawns on you one day that you are different. There will be other times when you know you are transforming and it is a very slow process and there will be times when you are transforming and it is happening lighting fast. Either way, it is important to keep transforming if you want to continue to be successful.

♛ GET RESULTS NOW! STEPS

1. Are you afraid of change?   Y or N

2. If so, was there an event in your past that contributed to it and if so, can you describe it?

   _____

   _____

   _____

   _____

3. If not, why not?

   _____

   _____

   _____

   _____

4. Are you ready to change that pattern and if so how?

   _____

   _____

   _____

   _____

5. Can you recognize when you are overwhelmed?   Y or N

6. When you are overwhelmed are you able to recognize that this means you are now at a new level of success?   Y or N

7. Are you able to start using the word "overloaded" and the word "overwhelmed" correctly?   Y or N

8. How are you planning to do that?

   _____

   _____

   _____

   _____

9. How will you recognize you have transformed?

   _____

   _____

   _____

   _____

10. Are you ready to transform and keep transforming?
    Y or N

CHAPTER 14

SUCCESS

"It takes a long time to climb the mountain so you better celebrate because you don't stay up at the top of that mountain that long."

Jean, The Results Queen®

Transformation brings you to the last stage in The RESULTS Formula . . . Success. The "S" in The RESULTS Formula stands for "Success." I like to take that one step further as I define success as a celebration, so I often say this stage is the Success Celebration phase.

It takes hard work to achieve success. For almost all, achieving success is worth every step. When you achieve success, the most important thing to do is celebrate. The problem is most people don't celebrate. What they do is either nothing and continue on the path or they just barely acknowledge what they did, and then they move forward.

There is a problem with that, and here it is. If we don't take the time to celebrate eventually, we start to feel like everything is just a grind. When things start to become a grind, we often don't want to do that activity anymore. What happens next is we stop, and often we stop way too soon. That's where celebrating comes in.

Why is it important to celebrate? I could explain it through brain chemistry, and the way dopamine works in our body. Instead, just know our brains need constant reinforcement of success. If we don't experience these "hits of success" as I call them, then our brains compel us to stop because our brains don't think we are successful. Our brains want us to do things we find pleasurable, and that is why we must celebrate our successes.

I suggest you celebrate both the small successes and the large successes. If you did something you thought was challenging and you were successful doing it then celebrate that success. If you land a large account or get a promotion, then celebrate that. For many of my clients, I ask them to celebrate after each 90-day plan.

As I said before, I believe having a 90-day plan is so important because it guides you through the success you want to achieve, and it gives you those milestones to reflect on to understand where you were, where you are now and where you want to be. Our brains need a memorable reference point, also called a reward, to make the whole journey worthwhile.

Ways to celebrate or reward yourself and/or your team includes a great dinner, a piece of jewelry, a new watch or even a new car. There are lots of ways to reward yourself. You could reward yourself with a cruise or a pizza party. It doesn't matter if it is an experience or a tangible item. What matters is your brain can recall the celebration and the success anchored to it.

Let me give you an example. I worked with a management team for four years until the company sold. Every 90 days, from the day we started working with them until the company sold, the management team not only created a new 90-day plan, but they also celebrated what they had achieved.

At the farewell party, the management team reviewed all their accomplishments along with every celebration. It wasn't a planned thing. They just started talking about the different events, the reasons why they were celebrating and the successes that went with them. Over the course of four years, they had 16 celebrations, one each quarter. They could remember each celebration in vivid detail. Can you remember what you did four years ago in vivid detail? How about last week? It was then I realized how impactful success celebrations could be and from that point on, I made sure all of my clients, my community and my team celebrated success.

I find so many of my clients don't celebrate success; they just stay in the grind. When they come to me, I am the one that celebrates their success, and I am often the one who teaches them to celebrate, both of which, I find so interesting. What makes success celebration so hard for us?

I believe the reason we find celebrating success so hard is due to the baggage we carry around from our past. I spoke about this baggage before. If you forgot, then let me remind you what I mean by baggage. Baggage is the beliefs and thoughts you have or more likely that others have given you. These are beliefs and thoughts you have decided to live by. The problem with baggage is it often doesn't serve you and doesn't help you achieve the success you want to achieve. It holds you back. It is limiting you and keeping you small. It is keeping you from living the life you were meant to live. Because we have lived with these beliefs, thoughts, feelings, etc. or what I call "baggage," for such a long time it has become so much a part of us we don't even realize how it is impacting us until someone else points it out! Here's the worst part of this, usually it's other people's baggage that we are carrying around. If you are still having trouble with this concept, go back to the OPB chapter in this book.

Know it is ok to have trouble with OPB. It takes a lot of time and effort to get rid of it. It is especially hard to get rid of it yourself.

When my clients come to me, it is me who points out the baggage they have been carrying not for years, but decades. Once my clients realize they even have baggage, we then start to figure out whose baggage it is and how and why my client decided to pick up those bags.

Unfortunately, baggage often comes from a parent trying to protect or compel my clients when they were children. Only when my clients understand where the baggage comes from, can we start to eliminate it. Remember I told you, my mentor, Alan Weiss would say, "It is time to throw that baggage off your train and get your own baggage."

Why is it important to speak about your baggage? It is important because it is most often this baggage that prevents us from success celebration. Things like:

- I can't toot my own horn
- No one will like me
- I will be judged
- I have to be humble
- You aren't perfect so who are you to celebrate?

Are you getting the idea of the baggage that my clients carry around with them? Are you getting the idea of what baggage you may be carrying around? Are you getting the idea of how this baggage is impacting your Success Celebration?

Here is another way for you to track success. I call it Signature Day™. What is a Signature Day? A Signature Day is where everything goes right and you document three things about the day that went right and how you made them right. You can write these things down on a paper calendar or in your electronic calendar. That part doesn't matter. What matters is you document what and the how.

Why does that matter? On the days that are not Signature Days, you can go back to a previous Signature Day, look at what you did and how you did it. This will give you some ideas of how to turn your day around so it gets better.

Why do I call these Signature Day? Think about how a great painter signs their name to a painting when the have completed the painting. They only sign their name when they are happy with the picture. I thought if a great painter can sign their name to their paintings, then why could I sign my name to the days that were really great?

I decided to give Signature Day a try. On the days that I hit it out of the park, I wrote down the three things I did and how I did them and then I signed my name. (I used a paper calendar at the time. I know use my electronic calendar).

I told my coach about what I was doing. He asked me to start tracking my Signature Days. What was interesting was that after a while I started having more Signature Days. These Signature Days turned into Signature Weeks. These Signature Weeks turned into Signature Months. These Signature Months turned into Signature Years.

When I am not up to my standards, I go back to see how many Signature Days I have in a row. If I don't have that many Signature Days, then I know that I need to look at The Results Formula. Am I ready? Do I have the end defined? Have I fully developed action steps? Am I being held accountable? Am I involved? I examine my Levels of Learning. I figure out where I am in the Transformation and I decide if I am celebrating my

Successes? I do the same things for my clients.

I take my clients through the same process. When they have success, the sign their name to the day and they celebrate. Too often we just don't celebrate.

This is why Success Celebration is so important. It is an anchor that helps our brains remember the successes we have achieved. You can pre-plan your celebration or be spontaneous once you have achieved success. Either way, celebrate every success no matter how big or small because this reinforces why it is necessary to continue on this lifelong RESULTS journey.

One last thing about Success. Include in your celebration some recovery time. What do I mean by recovery time? After you have run a marathon, you don't go and run another marathon, you take some time to recover. That means you rest. Even if you take an hour to rest, your body needs it.

How do you rest? Go on vacation. Lie in bed and read or watch movies. Go out and garden. Do something that allows your mind and body some time to recover so when you are ready to implement The RESULTS Formula again, you will be ready to go.

Success Celebrations can be small or large. They can happen daily, weekly, monthly or yearly depending on what the success is.

It doesn't matter. What matters is that you celebrate. It is a way to know you successful!

♔ GET RESULTS NOW! STEPS

1. Write down all of the ways you could celebrate success so when you get stuck and can't think of anything, you can look at this list.

    _____

    _____

    _____

2. What, if anything, would stop you from having a Success Celebration?

    _____

    _____

    _____

3. What will you do to overcome that so you can have a Success Celebration?

    _____

    _____

    _____

4. Who can help you make sure that you have Success Celebrations? (Make sure to tell this person what their responsibilities are).

    _____

    _____

    _____

CHAPTER 15

YOUR NEXT STEPS ON YOUR RESULTS JOURNEY

"The RESULTS Journey is never done if it is done right."

Jean, The Results Queen®

W hat is great about The RESULTS Formula is it is repeatable. Once you achieve the RESULTS Formula, you can get yourself ready for the next level of success. When you are "ready" you can begin to implement The RESULTS Formula over and over again. You never stop.

Many of us crave the next level of success, but few of us know how to achieve it. Now you have a proven formula you can use to obtain the ultimate success you are seeking.

There are some things that can get in the way of you and the RESULTS Formula. I want to make sure to point them out now so when they do come up, and they will, you will recognize them and deal with them directly so you can get back on your RESULTS journey.

There are a lot of challenges, obstacles and even people that will try to push you off your RESULTS journey. Being aware of that, in and of itself, is important. Knowing how to handle the challenges and actually handling them means you will always stay on your RESULTS Journey path. When you get pushed off your RESULTS Journey path, the most important thing to do is get right back on.

The biggest challenge is managing you. There is a lot going on with you. It is easy to get off track. It is easy to get lazy. It is easy to give up. To get successful, you have to fight for it. You have to commit and keep going. You must live with the ups and downs of life and not let these dips and valleys get to you. The RESULTS Formula is designed to assist you in making sure you can manage you. That's why I invented it. I wanted a way for everyone to be able to not only manage themselves, but to get themselves back on track when they fall off.

Getting back on track makes a difference in success outcomes.

Get comfortable being uncomfortable. There are times when this journey gets uncomfortable. There are things you are going to have to do that will make you uncomfortable. When you are comfortable being uncomfortable, there is nothing you can't handle.

Take my example of running. I started running, and I hate running. I was told that once I started, I would really like it and I would want to run more. I will tell you I still hate running. While I hate it, I keep doing it. Why? For me, it is about what I can achieve. Not everything I do is comfortable.

When you do get off track, because I know you will, go back on the RESULTS Formula. Ask yourself if you are ready. When you are, think about and write down your end result. Develop your action steps. Get you in gear and if you can't get in gear find someone who will help you. Notice your Levels of Learning. Document and keep track, so you can see the progress you are making. Pick a period of time and compare yourself to see how you have transformed. Finally, celebrate your success. I know you can do this.

It is now up to you.

Here is your proven RESULTS Formula.

Go use it!

👑 GET RESULTS NOW! STEPS

1. **Write down what you are going to do right now to get started with the Results Formula.**

_____

_____

_____

_____

_____

2. Think about and write down what could take you off your RESULTS Journey.

_____

_____

_____

_____

3. Identify how you will know that you are off track.

_____

_____

_____

_____

4. Write why you want to commit to using the Results Formula.

_____

_____

_____

_____

_____

5. What can you get by using the Results Formula?

_____

_____

_____

_____

THE LAST WORDS FROM JEAN, THE RESULTS QUEEN®

You can get results. More results. Better results. Different results. You just need to use the information in this book. My clients have used this information to grow both professionally and personally. If they can do it, so can you.

Drop me a line at jean@getmoreresults.com to let me know if I can help you.

Now go get more results!

To Your RESULTS!

Jean

The Results Queen®

ACKNOWLEDGEMENTS

This is the part I truly hate because I don't want to leave anyone out. There have been so many people who have helped me along the way, and it would take pages and pages to thank everyone by name.

Here is what I will say…thank you to YOU. You know who you are and I am grateful to what you have done for me from the bottom of my heart. Without you I would not be standing here. Thank you for walking beside me, listening to me, guiding me, hitting me with a 2x4 and giving me a kiss, but most of all thank you for being there when I needed you. Here's to you!!

ABOUT JEAN, THE RESULTS QUEEN®

Her clients crowned Jean Oursler as The Results Queen® because she is all about getting unprecedented RESULTS at unprecedented speed that creates and maintains unprecedented performance. Jean is one of the country's top business consultants, a top rated speaker as well as a world-class coach, and was rated by her Women Presidents Organization chapter members as the #1 facilitator in the world for 2016-2017 out of 150 facilitators across the globe.

To help her clients achieve more results Jean created the RESULTS! Formula. The RESULTS! Formula is easy to remember and easy to use. Jean and her Results Team use the RESULTS! Formula every day to achieve extraordinary growth rates for entrepreneurs, business owners, accountants, lawyers, and financial planners.

Jean's clients say, "Her no-nonsense approach is results-focused, completely personalized to meet the needs of you and your business and produces double digit growth". In addition to working with her clients, Jean also delivers workshops and keynote addresses. To talk to Jean about getting more results or to schedule a speaking engagement, please email her at jean@getmoreresults.com.

www.ingramcontent.com/pod-product-compliance
Lightning Source LLC
Chambersburg PA
CBHW060549200326
41521CB00007B/543